MISSOURI TRIVIA

MISSOURI TRIVIA

COMPILED BY
ERNIE COUCH

Rutledge Hill Press
Nashville, Tennessee

Published by Rutledge Hill Press, Inc.
513 Third Avenue South
Nashville, Tennessee 37210

Typography by D&T/Bailey Typography, Nashville, Tennessee

Library of Congress Cataloging-in-Publication Data

Couch, Ernie, 1949-
  Missouri trivia / compiled by Ernie Couch.
    p. cm.
  ISBN 1-55853-203-X
  1. Missouri—History—Miscellanea. I. Title.
F466.5.C68 1992   92-32523
977.8—dc20   CIP

Printed in the United States of America
1 2 3 4 5 6 7 8—99 98 97 96 95 94 93 92

PREFACE

Today Missouri stands as a unique blend of age old traditions steeped in hospitality and the latest in high-tech advancement. Missouri's colorful and compelling history speaks of a richly diversified land and people. Captured within these pages are some of the highlights of this rich heritage, both the known and the not so well known.

Missouri Trivia is designed to be informative, educational, and entertaining. But most of all I hope that you will be motivated to learn more about the great state of Missouri.

—Ernie Couch

To Homer and Jewel Sturdevant and
the great people of Missouri

TABLE OF CONTENTS

GEOGRAPHY

C H A P T E R   O N E

Q. In 1765 what town was made the capital of Upper Louisiana?

A. St. Louis.

———◆———

Q. What Barton County town was named in honor of a president of the Republic of Texas?

A. Lamar (for Mirabeau Buonaparte Lamar).

———◆———

Q. Where is the national headquarters of the Assemblies of God?

A. Springfield.

———◆———

Q. What is the southwesternmost county in the state?

A. McDonald.

———◆———

Q. Where was the outlaw Jesse James born on September 5, 1847?

A. Kearney.

Q. What is the U.S. Postal abbreviation for Missouri?

A. MO.

———◆———

Q. Where was Missouri's first normal school opened on September 2, 1867, by Prof. Joseph Baldwin?

A. Kirksville.

———◆———

Q. What town is at the geographical center of the state?

A. Miller.

———◆———

Q. Springfield consolidated with what rival town in 1887?

A. North Springfield.

———◆———

Q. What town, named for a St. Louis trader, was the seat of Bates County from 1848 to 1856?

A. Papinsville (for Melicourt Papin).

———◆———

Q. From 1840 to 1846 what town served as the seat of Buchanan County?

A. Sparta.

———◆———

Q. Robidoux's Post evolved into what Missouri city?

A. St. Joseph.

Q. Where did thirty-one-year-old Abraham Lincoln woo Mary Todd in 1840?

A. Columbia.

———◆———

Q. In what southern county is the community of Blue Eye?

A. Stone.

———◆———

Q. What is the capital of Missouri?

A. Jefferson City.

———◆———

Q. Murphysburg and Joplin City were incorporated under what name in 1872 before being re-incorporated by the legislature in 1873 as the city of Joplin?

A. Union City.

———◆———

Q. How many states border Missouri?

A. Eight.

———◆———

Q. Based on the 1990 census, what is the least populated county in the state?

A. Worth.

———◆———

Q. Which north Missouri town has been called the City of the Maples?

A. Macon.

Q. Advertised as a future metropolis, what now long abandoned Mississippi River town site was founded in 1835 by Col. William Muldrow?

A. Marion City.

———◆———

Q. The courthouse of what county was chosen to represent Missouri courthouses in the 1939 New York World's Fair?

A. Ralls.

———◆———

Q. What was the name of Rep. James "Champ" Beauchamp Clark's home in Bowling Green?

A. Honey Shuck.

———◆———

Q. In what time zone is Missouri situated?

A. Central.

———◆———

Q. What St. Louis suburb was known by such early names as Village à Robert and Marais des Liards?

A. Bridgeton

———◆———

Q. With Cooper County's formation in 1818, what town became the county seat?

A. Boonville.

———◆———

Q. For what western frontier explorer was Pike County named?

A. Brig. Gen. Zebulon Montgomery Pike.

Q. What Missouri city bears the name of a frontier Methodist minister?

A. Joplin (for Rev. Harris G. Joplin).

Q. The community of Couch is in what county?

A. Oregon.

Q. What Missouri town is known as Redbud City?

A. Nevada.

Q. The native American word for catfish is the name of what eastern Missouri river?

A. The Meramec.

Q. Near what present-day town in 1798 did Rev. John Clark preach the first Protestant sermon in Missouri?

A. Herculaneum.

Q. What southeastern Warren County community was platted by John Young in 1817?

A. Marthasville.

Q. For whom is Keytesville, the seat of Chariton County, named?

A. Rev. James Keyte.

Q. Where in 1715 did governor general Sieur Antoine de la Mothe Cadillac open Missouri's first lead "diggin's"?

A. Mine La Motte.

Q. In which county is Missouri's own Atlanta situated?

A. Macon.

Q. The Creole word meaning "copper" is the name of what Missouri river?

A. The Cuivre.

Q. Where in 1805 was the first Sunday school west of the Mississippi organized and taught by Sarah Barton Murphy?

A. Farmington.

Q. Named the Festhalle, where may the world's largest wine hall be seen?

A. Hermann.

Q. The Des Moines River forms the northeast border of what county?

A. Clark.

Q. Where is Missouri's largest Amish community?

A. Jamesport.

Q. In 1935 what northern Missouri town drew national attention by electing women to fill all civic offices?

A. Greentop.

———◆———

Q. Concordia Seminary is in what St. Louis suburb?

A. Clayton.

———◆———

Q. From 1864 to 1878 what was the seat of Scott County?

A. Commerce.

———◆———

Q. What town in Webster County is named for the Massachusetts home of Daniel Webster?

A. Marshfield.

———◆———

Q. In what town is the Civil War Museum of Jackson County?

A. Lone Jack.

———◆———

Q. What Pemisco County town was named in honor of a Madison County lawyer and judge?

A. Caruthersville (for Samuel Caruthers).

———◆———

Q. Near what present-day town was the first Methodist church west of the Mississippi organized around 1806?

A. Jackson.

Q. What are the only two Missouri towns under which railroad tunnels have been constructed?

A. Freeburg and Gray Summit.

———◆———

Q. From what town was the seat of Macon County moved in 1863?

A. Bloomington.

———◆———

Q. What Pike County town was named by settlers from Kentucky for their former hometown?

A. Bowling Green.

———◆———

Q. Where is the History Museum of the Missouri Historical Society?

A. St. Louis.

———◆———

Q. The pony express's co-founder William H. Russell is buried in what town?

A. Palmyra.

———◆———

Q. What Boone County town was named for its midway location on the North Missouri Railroad between St. Louis and Ottumwa, Iowa?

A. Centralia.

———◆———

Q. Where did George G. Vest deliver his famous "Eulogy to the Dog" during the 1870 "Old Drum" trial?

A. Warrensburg.

Q. Father Helias d'Huddeghem named what Osage County community for the many clear springs he found in the area?

A. Rich Fountain.

———◆———

Q. Where did Col. Frederick William Blees establish the Blees Military Academy in 1875?

A. Macon.

———◆———

Q. What town's old stone jail now houses the Bushwhacker Museum?

A. Nevada.

———◆———

Q. Dr. E. G. Latham's suggestion, Vie Anna, was corrupted into what name for the seat of Maries County?

A. Vienna.

———◆———

Q. In what town is the Lewis and Clark Center?

A. St. Charles.

———◆———

Q. Maj. Christopher Clark named what Missouri county in honor of the North Carolina county in which he was born, and for the Kentucky county in which he had lived for several years?

A. Lincoln.

———◆———

Q. What Maries County town was named for a French resort?

A. Vichy.

Q. A nearby buffalo lick led to the naming of what town in Texas County?

A. Licking.

———◆———

Q. What southeastern Missouri town was founded in 1896 and named for a cashier at the Bank of Paragould, Arkansas?

A. Cardwell (for Frank Cardwell).

———◆———

Q. Where is the J. C. Penney Museum?

A. Hamilton.

———◆———

Q. Joshua N. Robbins named what Lincoln County community for a New York town?

A. Troy.

———◆———

Q. Laid out in 1858, what is the seat of Howell County?

A. West Plains.

———◆———

Q. Liberty Memorial, which is the only major museum in the nation focusing on World War I, is in what city?

A. Kansas City.

———◆———

Q. Covering 1,159 square miles, what is the largest county in Missouri?

A. Texas.

Q. What Mississippi River island did Missouri lose to Illinois in a boundary dispute?

A. Arsenal Island.

———◆———

Q. Bluff Grove and Lomax's Store were two early names of what Grundy County town?

A. Trenton.

———◆———

Q. Where was pony express rider and army scout Calamity Jane born in 1850?

A. Princeton.

———◆———

Q. "The big town where we live" is the meaning of what Shawnee place-name in Livingston County?

A. Chillicothe.

———◆———

Q. Where did Maj. Alvan Lightburne build his twenty-six-room mansion in 1852?

A. Liberty.

———◆———

Q. What town served as Missouri's first capital from 1821 to 1826?

A. St. Charles.

———◆———

Q. Near what town was Gen. John J. Pershing born on September 13, 1860?

A. Laclede.

Q. Measuring approximately seventy-six feet in length, the Sandy Creek Covered Bridge is in what county?

A. Jefferson.

———◆———

Q. What is the seat of Texas County?

A. Houston.

———◆———

Q. Prior to 1848, Waverly was known by what name?

A. Middletown.

———◆———

Q. What Saline County town is named for a former chief justice of the U.S. Supreme Court?

A. Marshall (for John Marshall).

———◆———

Q. Numerous salt springs led to the name of what county?

A. Saline.

———◆———

Q. Which county was named in honor of a delegate who died during the Constitutional Convention of 1820 at St. Louis?

A. Ray (for John Ray).

———◆———

Q. Where was Harry S Truman born on May 8, 1884?

A. Lamar.

Q. In eastern Greene County, what town developed on lands that were formerly part of a Kickapoo Indian reservation?

A. Strafford.

———◆———

Q. Greenville was the first name given to what Missouri River town?

A. Miami.

———◆———

Q. Housed in an 1892 Victorian mansion, the Museum of Ozarks' History is in what city?

A. Springfield.

———◆———

Q. What county, organized January 2, 1833, was named for a signer of the Declaration of Independence?

A. Carroll (for Charles Carroll).

———◆———

Q. In 1851 Rockport succeeded what settlement as the seat of Atchison County?

A. Linden.

———◆———

Q. What is the distance from Missouri's northern border to its southern border?

A. 285 miles.

———◆———

Q. Prior to 1839, Platte City was known by what name?

A. Martinville.

Q. What Nodaway County town was named in honor of the first white woman to live within the limits of the settlement?

A. Maryville (for Mary Graham).

———◆———

Q. Compared with the other states, where does Missouri rank in land area?

A. Seventeenth.

———◆———

Q. "Walnut" or "a place where walnuts grow" is the meaning of what native American place-name in Atchison County?

A. Tarkio.

———◆———

Q. By what name did Spanish authorities call Florissant?

A. St. Ferdinand.

———◆———

Q. What name was given to the 1837 land acquisition that created the northwest area of the state?

A. The Platte Purchase.

———◆———

Q. Where in Missouri did representatives of nineteen native American tribes sign treaties with U.S. commissioners in 1815?

A. Portage Des Sioux.

———◆———

Q. What is the northwesternmost county in the state?

A. Atchison.

Q. Versailles replaced what now-extinct town as the seat of Morgan County in 1833?

A. Millville.

Q. Missouri is how many times the size of Rhode Island?

A. Fifty-seven.

Q. In 1820 weekly stagecoach service was established between St. Charles and what settlement to the west?

A. Franklin.

Q. What is the meaning of the French abbreviation "aux-Arcs" from which *Ozarks* evolved?

A. "To Arkansas."

Q. Where was radical prohibition activist Carry A. Nation buried in 1911?

A. Belton.

Q. What was the childhood home of military administrator and diplomat Enoch Herbert Crowder?

A. Edinburg.

Q. How many townships are there in Missouri?

A. 329.

Q. Though Branson has been compared to Nashville, Tennessee, for its country music, in what county is Missouri's own Nashville situated?

A. Barton.

———◆———

Q. To what town did Mark Twain move with his parents in 1839?

A. Hannibal.

———◆———

Q. What Cass County town is said to have been named by a group of spiritualists led by Mrs. Jane Hawkins?

A. Peculiar.

———◆———

Q. G. H. Walser founded what community in Barton County in 1880 for free-thinkers?

A. Liberal.

———◆———

Q. What town in St. Charles County is named for a nineteenth-century St. Louis capitalist and railroad baron?

A. O'Fallon (for Maj. John O'Fallon).

———◆———

Q. In 1924, Montgomery City replaced what town as the seat of Montgomery County?

A. Danville.

———◆———

Q. Virtually all of the eastern boundary of Missouri is defined by what river?

A. The Mississippi.

Q. The community of Chain of Rocks is in what county?

A. Lincoln.

❖

Q. What southern Dunklin County town is named for the wife of the community's first postmaster?

A. Senath (for Senath Hale Douglas).

❖

Q. Where was the notorious outlaw Belle Starr born in 1846?

A. Carthage.

❖

Q. What is the meaning of the native American place-name Mineola in Montgomery County?

A. "Healing waters."

❖

Q. In 1887 a gold and silver scam brought a temporary boom to what McDonald County community?

A. Splitlog.

❖

Q. What town replaced Franklin as the seat of Howard County in 1823?

A. Fayette.

❖

Q. According to Mormon teaching, at what site on Grand River in Daviess County did Adam give a final blessing to such patriarchs as Seth, Jared, Enoch, and Methuselah?

A. Adam-Ondi-Ahman.

Q. Before 1874 Bloomsdale was known by what name?

A. La Fourche à Duclos.

Q. In 1839 Martin Stephan led 600 Saxon Lutheran emigrants in the founding of what Perry County town?

A. Altenburg.

Q. What Jasper County town is named for an ancient North African trade center?

A. Carthage.

Q. Where are the state headquarters of the Daughters of the American Revolution?

A. Boonville.

Q. The 1861 stand-off of Callaway County residents and Union forces led to what nickname for the county?

A. The Kingdom.

Q. What Dunklin County town was named for a Massachusetts community?

A. Malden.

Q. William ("Bloody Bill") Anderson and his Confederate raiders called what central Missouri town their "capital"?

A. Rocheport.

Q. James Alcorn laid out what Howard County community in 1828?

A. New Franklin.

———◆———

Q. What village, founded by a small group of Creoles in 1800, stood within the limits of present-day Fredericktown?

A. St. Michael.

———◆———

Q. According to tradition, Tanglefoot was the original name of what Jefferson County town which was platted in 1878?

A. Festus.

———◆———

Q. What is the major airport that serves St. Louis?

A. Lambert-St. Louis International Airport.

———◆———

Q. In 1845 the bodies of Daniel and Rebecca Boone were moved from their original burial site near Dutzow to what out-of-state city?

A. Frankfort, Kentucky.

———◆———

Q. What county has been called the Mother of Counties?

A. Howard County.

———◆———

Q. What Lafayette County town was laid out in 1836 under the name of Poston's Landing?

A. Napoleon.

Q. Thomas C. Fletcher, the state's first Missouri-born governor, was a native of what town?

A. Herculaneum.

———◆———

Q. In 1821 what central Missouri town was the head of the Santa Fe Trail?

A. Franklin.

———◆———

Q. Where is Northwest Missouri State University?

A. Maryville.

———◆———

Q. Constructed on the bank of the Missouri River in 1869, what was the name of riverboat magnate Capt. Joseph Kinney's mansion?

A. Rivercene.

———◆———

Q. What nickname has been applied to the southeastern corner of the state?

A. Boot Heel.

———◆———

Q. The Fountain City is the title given to what southern Jefferson County town?

A. De Soto.

———◆———

Q. What Washington County town was named for a silver mining city in Mexico?

A. Potosi (for San Luis Potosi).

Q. Where was the first land battle of the Civil War to take place in Missouri fought on June 17, 1861?

A. South of Boonville.

Q. From 1829 to 1833 Arrow Rock was known by what name?

A. New Philadelphia.

Q. Where in 1914 did the St. Louis Council of the Boy Scouts of America establish a camp?

A. Irondale.

Q. Daniel Boone's youngest son, Nathan, settled and named what Greene County community?

A. Ash Grove.

Q. Near what present-day town was the first Presbyterian service held in Missouri on December 1, 1807?

A. Caledonia.

Q. How many Missouri counties, along with ten Iowa counties, were created, at least in part, from Howard County?

A. Thirty-six.

Q. The Missouri Lumber and Mining Company founded what southern Carter County town in 1887?

A. Grandin.

Q. What is the meaning of the two Algonquin words *misi* and *sipi* from which Mississippi County and the river derive their name?

A. "Big water."

———◆———

Q. In 1859 Alton succeeded what town as the seat of Ripley County?

A. Thomasville.

———◆———

Q. What Saline County community was at one time known as the Saratoga of the West?

A. Sweet Springs.

———◆———

Q. Where was a home for Confederate veterans established in 1891?

A. Higginsville.

———◆———

Q. In what Independence cemetery is fur trader, frontiersman, and army scout James Bridger buried?

A. Mount Washington Memorial Cemetery.

———◆———

Q. What was the first name applied to Odessa?

A. Kirkpatrick.

———◆———

Q. Near what community did Daniel Boone die at his son's home on September 26, 1820?

A. Defiance.

Q. What county was named in honor of a state legislator from St. Charles County?

A. Audrain (for Col. James H. Audrain).

———◆———

Q. The Berlin Emigration Society founded what Warren County community in 1832?

A. Dutzow.

———◆———

Q. What was the first seat of Pike County?

A. Louisiana.

———◆———

Q. From 1880 to 1900 what was the largest town in Miller County?

A. Aurora Springs.

———◆———

Q. Although first called Mount Pleasant, what St. Charles County community was renamed to honor the wife of Leonard Harold, who had laid out the town?

A. Augusta.

———◆———

Q. Where in Marion County was the world's first Masonic college established in 1844?

A. Philadephia.

———◆———

Q. Fulton was first known by what name which honored a French historian and philosopher?

A. Volney (for Count Constantin-François Volney).

Q. Ranked as the tallest monument constructed in the United States, exactly how tall is the Gateway Arch in St. Louis?

A. 630 feet.

Q. In what Missouri community was the great American humorist Mark Twain born on November 30, 1835?

A. Florida.

Q. From what town did Ulysses S. Grant and his troops rout Confederate forces on July 11, 1861, without bloodshed on either side?

A. Monroe City.

Q. What Missouri town was named in honor of Andrew Jackson's home in Tennessee?

A. Hermitage.

Q. What town situated near the mouth of the Grand River was named in 1836 for an English community?

A. Brunswick (for Brunswick Terrace).

Q. Before being renamed in 1843 in honor of Charles Pratt, Earl of Camden, Camden County was known by what name?

A. Kinderhook County.

Q. Platted in 1835, what was the second settlement to be established in Lafayette County?

A. Dover.

Q. Because of the county's original vast land area, what nickname was given to Ray County?

A. Free State of Ray.

———✦———

Q. What Jackson County town was named in honor of a surveyor of the Santa Fe Trail and factor at Fort Osage?

A. Sibley (for Maj. George C. Sibley).

———✦———

Q. The Reorganized Church of Jesus Christ of Latter Day Saints is headquartered in what city?

A. Independence.

———✦———

Q. What two Missouri counties were named in honor of the seventh president of the United States?

A. Jackson and Hickory, for Andrew ("Old Hickory") Jackson.

———✦———

Q. Prior to 1880, New Cambria was known by what name?

A. Stockton.

———✦———

Q. What Shelby County town is said to have been named by railroad conductor John Duff for one of his children?

A. Clarence.

———✦———

Q. What Macon County town has the same name as a Peruvian seaport?

A. Callao.

Q. Where did the Hannibal and St. Joseph Railroad locate its shops and roundhouses in 1859?

A. Brookfield.

Q. On December 29, 1836, what county was established by the Missouri legislature as a Mormon refuge?

A. Caldwell.

Q. The area that became the St. Louis suburb of Maplewood was known by what name prior to 1890?

A. Sutton.

Q. In what town is the Benton County Museum, which is housed in an 1886 school building?

A. Warsaw.

Q. By what name did early Missouri history writers refer to the Fabius River?

A. The Jeffron or Jeffreon.

Q. The seat of Ray County is named for what Virginia city?

A. Richmond.

Q. When Brentwood was incorporated in 1896, what two other subdivisions merged with the St. Louis suburb?

A. Berry Place and Maddenville.

Q. What town is at the confluence of the Wyaconda and Mississippi rivers?

A. La Grange.

———◆———

Q. The Osage word for "clear water" is the name of what Newton County town?

A. Neosho.

———◆———

Q. What St. Louis County town was named for a one-time U.S. consul to Venezuela?

A. Ellisville (for Vespuccio Ellis).

———◆———

Q. Union succeeded what settlement in 1826 as the seat of Franklin County?

A. Newport.

———◆———

Q. What is the oldest lead- and zinc-mining town in southwestern Missouri?

A. Grandy.

———◆———

Q. During the mid-1800s what northeast Missouri town almost rivaled St. Louis and Chicago in pork processing?

A. Alexandria.

———◆———

Q. Where was former First Lady Bess Wallace Truman born on February 13, 1885?

A. Independence.

Q. A blackjack tree that served as a landmark on the prairie in southeast Jackson County was the source of what town's name?

A. Lone Jack.

———◆———

Q. In 1847 what Moniteau County settlement was renamed California?

A. Boonesborough.

———◆———

Q. What town in northeast Caldwell County is named for the vice president under Buchanan?

A. Breckenridge (for John C. Breckenridge).

———◆———

Q. Although an early spelling error was never corrected, what town was named in honor of Dr. Pleasant Lea?

A. Lees Summit.

———◆———

Q. The Missouri State Industrial School for Girls is in what town?

A. Chillicothe.

———◆———

Q. What St. Louis suburb was named for a chief engineer of the Missouri Pacific Railroad?

A. Kirkwood (for James P. Kirkwood).

———◆———

Q. Long stretches of I-44 and U.S. 66 follow the approximate route of what early stage and military trail?

A. Old Wire Road.

Q. What town, settled by B. J. Inge in 1843, was originally known as Traveler's Repose?

A. St. Clair.

———◆———

Q. Founded in 1886, Mountain Grove evolved out of what earlier settlement that relocated to the present town site in 1883?

A. Hickory Springs.

———◆———

Q. What Clark County town derived its name from a corruption of the name of the Gawakie tribe?

A. Kahoka.

———◆———

Q. In 1850 what town was founded to serve as the seat of newly formed Butler County?

A. Poplar Bluff.

———◆———

Q. Mount Helicon was the original name of what eastern Missouri town?

A. Sullivan.

———◆———

Q. Where is the Adrain County Historical Society Museum?

A. Kirksville.

———◆———

Q. In 1857, M. W. Trask and W. H. Ferguson surveyed what town site in Crawford County?

A. Cuba.

Q. Van Buren, the present seat of Carter County, was formerly the seat of what county?

A. Ripley.

———◆———

Q. A large tree near the settlement's first post office gave what name to a Shannon County community?

A. Birch Tree.

———◆———

Q. Around 1900 approximately 100 Italian families, who came to Missouri via Arkansas, founded what Phelps County community?

A. Rosati (for Bishop Joseph Rosati).

———◆———

Q. Mississippi County was created from what county on February 14, 1845?

A. Scott.

———◆———

Q. Where is the Coal Miner's Museum?

A. Novinger.

———◆———

Q. What now nonexistent Mormon town in Caldwell County grew to a population of more than 4,000 within a year of its founding in 1836?

A. Far West.

———◆———

Q. During its first year, the town of St. James was known by what name?

A. Scioto.

Q. What small community was absorbed by the formation of Bennett Spring State Park?

A. Brice.

———◆———

Q. According to tradition, the name of the town Rolla is based on a spelling of early settler George Coppedge's odd pronunciation of what North Carolina city?

A. Raleigh.

———◆———

Q. During the Civil War what Vernon County town was known as the Bushwhackers' Capital?

A. Nevada.

———◆———

Q. Poplar Bluff is situated on what river?

A. The Black.

———◆———

Q. What is the easternmost county in the state?

A. Mississippi.

———◆———

Q. Col. Nathan Boone and his wife, Olive Van Bibber Boone, are buried near what community?

A. Ash Grove.

———◆———

Q. Moore and Butler are early names of what Dunklin County town?

A. Kennett.

Q. Featuring original mid-nineteenth century structures, Missouri Town 1855 is found in what Kansas City suburb?

A. Blue Springs.

———◆———

Q. What river forms the northern portion of Missouri's western border?

A. The Missouri.

———◆———

Q. For a few months in 1839–40 what community served as the temporary seat of Saline County?

A. Arrow Rock.

———◆———

Q. What town has a French name that means "flowering"?

A. Florissant.

———◆———

Q. The state of Missouri contains how many square miles?

A. 69,686.

———◆———

Q. What county is named for a Revolutionary War patriot who was killed in the battle of Bunker Hill?

A. Warren (for Gen. Joseph Warren).

———◆———

Q. In a boundary dispute with Kentucky, what Mississippi River island did Missouri lose?

A. Wolf Island.

ENTERTAINMENT

C H A P T E R T W O

Q. The popular musical comedy *The Unsinkable Molly Brown* was based on the life of what Hannibal native?

A. Margaret Tobin Brown.

◆

Q. What circus was based out of Lancaster in the late 1800s?

A. Col. Billy Hall's Circus.

◆

Q. Where did Cab Calloway apply for his first musicians' union card?

A. Kansas City.

◆

Q. What famous fan dancer was born near Cross Timbers in 1903?

A. Sally Rand.

◆

Q. Where was country music star Porter Wagoner born on August 12, 1930?

A. West Plains.

Q. What Missourian had the 1974 crossover hit record "I Can Help"?

A. Billy Swan.

—————◆—————

Q. Shelley Winters, who was born in St. Louis, played what role in the motion picture *Bloody Mama?*

A. Ma Barker.

—————◆—————

Q. Missouri-born jazz musician Coleman Hawkins appeared in one episode of what successful 1960s television series?

A. "Route 66."

—————◆—————

Q. What Green Ridge-born actress was the star of the silent screen cliffhanger series *The Perils of Pauline?*

A. Pearl White.

—————◆—————

Q. The country-gospel group White River is based in what town?

A. Ozark.

—————◆—————

Q. What is Branson's original country music and comedy stage show?

A. *Presley's Mountain Music Jubilee.*

—————◆—————

Q. Where was motion picture and television producer/writer/ director Robert Altman born on February 20, 1925?

A. Kansas City.

Q. What Missouri-born actor starred in the television series "Naked City," "Mr. Novack," and "Longstreet"?

A. James Franciscus.

Q. What rage of Broadway and Paris music halls during the late 1920s and early 1930s was born in St. Louis on June 3, 1906?

A. Josephine Baker.

Q. Under what name did Missouri-born country performer Ferlin Husky team up with Jean Shepard to record the 1952 hit "Dear John Letter"?

A. Terry Preston.

Q. Where was long-time CBS news anchor Walter Cronkite born in 1916?

A. St. Joseph.

Q. What violent 1978 comedy starring Christopher Mitchum was filmed in St. Louis?

A. *Stingray.*

Q. St. Louis-born actor Vincent Price appeared in what 1961 horror movie based on an Edgar Allan Poe story?

A. *The Pit and the Pendulum.*

Q. On what label did Kansas City-born tenor saxophonist Harold Kenneth Asby record his 1972 "Born to Swing" album?

A. Jazz Master.

Q. What independent 1987 horror movie was directed and produced by St. Louisian Jerry Koch?

A. *Gun's Eye*.

———◆———

Q. Missouri-born actor Dick Van Dyke played opposite Julie Andrews in what 1964 Disney motion picture?

A. *Mary Poppins*.

———◆———

Q. How many spectators crowded aboard the showboat *Floating Palace* when it stopped at St. Louis in 1852?

A. 2,500.

———◆———

Q. The 1974 film version of Mark Twain's classic *Tom Sawyer* was primarily shot in and around what community?

A. Arrow Rock.

———◆———

Q. In what 1942 movie did St. Louis actress Katherine Vincent make her screen debut?

A. *Peptipa's Waltz*.

———◆———

Q. Trumpet player John ("Yank") Lawson, who worked with the successful bands of Bob Crosby, Tommy Dorsey, and Benny Goodman, was born in what town?

A. Trenton.

———◆———

Q. What Kansas City-born blues singer and composer became known by the nickname Big Joe?

A. Joseph Vernon Turner.

Q. Where were the Jordanaires organized in 1948?

A. Springfield.

———◆———

Q. *It Happened One Night, The Grapes of Wrath,* and *The Glenn Miller Story* are some of the more than 200 movies in which what Missourian appeared?

A. Irving Bacon.

———◆———

Q. Musician/composer Burt Bacharach was born in what Missouri city on May 12, 1928?

A. Kansas City.

———◆———

Q. "Peyton Place" and "All My Children" are both television credits of what actress from St. Joseph?

A. Ruth Warrick.

———◆———

Q. By what stage name was De Soto-born country comedian and banjo player Benjamin Francis ("Whitey") Ford best known?

A. The Duke of Paducah.

———◆———

Q. What Stephens College student went on to play the role of Mary Ann in the television series "Gilligan's Island"?

A. Dawn Wells.

———◆———

Q. Where is the annual Bluegrass Pickin' Time held?

A. Dixon.

Q. What Kansas Citian became a nationally known cowboy star in the 1949 motion picture *Red Rider?*

A. Jim Bannon.

———◆———

Q. Pianist Jess Alexandria Stacy, who gained national fame with Benny Goodman's orchestra from 1935 to 1939, was born in what community?

A. Bird's Point.

———◆———

Q. Television actor Scott Bakula attended what St. Louis high school?

A. Kirkwood High School.

———◆———

Q. What Missouri bass player and singer performed in such movies as *New Orleans, High Society,* and *The Glenn Miller Story?*

A. Arvell Shaw.

———◆———

Q. The Ozark Mountain Daredevils evolved out of what country-rock band?

A. Cosmic Corncob and His Amazing Mountain Daredevils.

———◆———

Q. What 1983 ABC television movie depicted the nuclear destruction of Kansas City?

A. *The Day After.*

———◆———

Q. Country singer Jan Howard was born in what town on March 13, 1932?

A. West Plains.

Q. What highly successful country music television show, with Red Foley as host, made its network debut from Springfield in 1955?

A. "Ozark Jubilee."

Q. In 1968 St. Louis-born musician Callen Radcliffe ("Cal") Tjader co-founded what record label?

A. Skye Records.

Q. What Kansas City native became known as the first of the modern jazz flutists?

A. Frank Wellington Wess.

Q. Missouri-born Jane Wyman won an Academy Award for best actress for her role in what 1948 movie?

A. *Johnny Belinda.*

Q. In what 1974–75 television series did David Hartman play the role of an English teacher at Harry S Truman Memorial High School in Webster Groves?

A. "Lucas Tanner."

Q. Some scenes from what 1936 movie were shot at the Missouri State Penitentiary in Jefferson City?

A. *The Voice of Bugle Ann.*

Q. Along with trumpeter Dizzy Gillespie, what Kansas City-born alto saxophonist was responsible for the rise of bebop?

A. Charlie Parker.

Q. In what 1957 motion picture did Kansas City actor John Ashley make his screen debut?

A. *Dragstrip Girl.*

Q. Where is the American Folk Music Festival held?

A. Silver Dollar City, Branson.

Q. Missouri native Narvel Felts had what number-one hit in 1975?

A. "Reconsider Baby."

Q. Actor George C. Scott attended what Missouri college?

A. University of Missouri, Columbia.

Q. What St. Louis native played the part of Scarlett's mother, Mrs. O'Hara, in the 1939 classic *Gone With the Wind?*

A. Barbara O'Neal.

Q. By age fifteen, country singer Leona Williams had her own show on what Jefferson City radio station?

A. KWOS.

Q. The Benji movie series was directed by what St. Louis native?

A. Joe Camp.

Q. Kemper Military School and College in Boonville, Van Horn High School in Independence, and the Liberty town square were all locations for the filming of what 1986 NBC movie?

A. *Combat High.*

———◆———

Q. What Kansas Citian appeared in the horror movie *Dracula's Daughter?*

A. Marguerite Churchill.

———◆———

Q. While leading a small band in Kansas City in 1936, what jazz pianist was "discovered" by talent scout John Hammond?

A. Count Basie.

———◆———

Q. In 1951, Missouri native Dennis Weaver made his Broadway debut in what production?

A. *Come Back Little Sheba.*

———◆———

Q. Teddy and Doyle, the Wilburn Brothers, were born in what southern Missouri town?

A. Thayer.

———◆———

Q. What Kansas Citian achieved international eminence while playing tenor saxophone with the Duke Ellington orchestra from 1939 to 1943?

A. Benjamin Francis ("Ben") Webster.

———◆———

Q. The long-running television series "Bonanza" was written, produced, and directed by what Kansas Citian?

A. Robert Altman.

Q. What actor, born in St. Louis in 1898, was a victim of the Hollywood blacklists of the McCarthy era?

A. Morris Carnovsky.

Q. The popular television series "Designing Women" and "Evening Shade" were created by what Missouri native?

A. Linda Bloodworth-Thomason.

Q. Pioneer jazz organist William Strethen ("Wild Bill") Davis was born in what town in 1918?

A. Glasgow.

Q. What featured actor in the television series "Our Miss Brooks" was born in St. Louis on October 2, 1913?

A. William Ching.

Q. Actress Jill Eikenberry grew up in what Missouri city?

A. St. Joseph.

Q. In 1960 Missouri-born producer/director Richard M. Gillaspy received an Emmy for his work in televising what political debate?

A. The Nixon-Khrushchev debate.

Q. What actor from Joplin appeared in such movies as *Arkansas Traveler, Madam X, The Sound and the Fury,* and *Ten Who Dared?*

A. John Beal.

Q. Where was country singer Helen Cornelius born on December 6, 1950?

A. Hannibal.

———◆———

Q. What Springfield-born musical director/composer has written for more than forty Disney features and scores of television programs?

A. Buddy Baker.

———◆———

Q. Actor Tom Berenger, who attended the University of Missouri, Columbia, made his screen debut in what 1977 motion picture?

A. *The Sentinel.*

———◆———

Q. What was the title of the Dillards' first album for Elektra Records?

A. "Back Porch Bluegrass."

———◆———

Q. Jazz alto saxophonist Theodore Guy ("Ted") Buckner was born in what city in 1913?

A. St. Louis.

———◆———

Q. What Missourian directed Laurel and Hardy in many of their screen roles?

A. Lewis R. Foster.

———◆———

Q. Mary Frann of "Days of Our Lives" and "Newhart" worked as a weather reporter at what St. Louis television station?

A. KSDK-TV.

Q. Where did actor John Goodman attend college?

A. Southwest Missouri State University.

———◆———

Q. *The Girl from Missouri, Hell's Angels, Public Enemy Number One, Platinum Blonde,* and *Bombshell* are all film credits of what Missouri-born actress?

A. Jean Harlow.

———◆———

Q. What vocalist who worked with Stan Kenton in the 1950s was born in Kansas City on November 8, 1927?

A. Chris Connor.

———◆———

Q. Stuntman Larry Holt is a native of what Missouri city?

A. Joplin.

———◆———

Q. What group is featured at Bob-O-Links Country Hoedown in Branson?

A. The Texans.

———◆———

Q. Where was actor Don Johnson born on December 15, 1950?

A. Flatt Creek.

———◆———

Q. What producer/writer, a native of Independence, has been associated with such successful television productions as "The Beverly Hillbillies," "Petticoat Junction," and "Green Acres"?

A. Paul Henning.

Q. Born in St. Louis in 1947, Kevin Kline received an Academy Award in 1989 for best supporting actor in what motion picture?

A. *A Fish Called Wanda.*

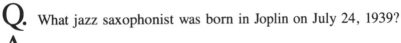

Q. What co-star of the adventure movie *Indiana Jones and the Temple of Doom* attended the University of Missouri, Columbia?

A. Kate Capshaw (Kathy Mail).

Q. The life story of what Kansas City-born actress was portrayed by Kim Novak in a 1957 motion picture?

A. Jeanne Eagels.

Q. What jazz saxophonist was born in Joplin on July 24, 1939?

A. Charles McPherson.

Q. Actress Irene Dunne attended what St. Louis school?

A. Loretta Academy.

Q. What Missouri native was the voice of Jiminy Cricket in Walt Disney's 1940 full-length animated movie *Pinocchio?*

A. Cliff Edwards.

Q. Under what name did Eva Sue McKee of Nevada record several country-pop hits during the 1960s and 1970s?

A. Sue Thompson.

Q. What popular screen villain from Kansas City made his film debut in 1911?

A. Fred Kohler.

———◆———

Q. Known for his silent comedy films, St. Louis-born director F. Richard Jones directed what single sound movie in 1930?

A. *Bulldog Drummond.*

———◆———

Q. What Pattonville-born actress married hockey star Wayne Gretsky in 1988?

A. Janet Jones.

———◆———

Q. Born in St. Louis in 1906, jazz clarinetist Charles Elsworth Russell was known by what nickname?

A. Pee Wee.

———◆———

Q. What country music publishing company was founded by the Wilburn Brothers?

A. Surefire Music.

———◆———

Q. *Tarzan and the Amazons* and *Tarzan's Magic Fountain* featured what "B feature" leading lady from Kansas City?

A. Brenda Joyce.

———◆———

Q. What 1980 motion picture starring Kurt Russell was shot in St. Louis?

A. *Escape from New York.*

Q. In 1946 what St. Joseph-born actress received the Donelson Award for best musical comedy performance for her role in *Spoon River Anthology?*

A. Betty Garrett.

———◆———

Q. What film and television star was born in West Plains on December 18, 1925?

A. Dick Van Dyke.

———◆———

Q. Virginia Katherine McMath is the actual name of what actress/dancer from Missouri?

A. Ginger Rogers.

———◆———

Q. What star of Charlie Chaplin's 1940 satire *The Great Dictator* was born in Sedalia on November 12, 1903?

A. Jack Okie.

———◆———

Q. In 1955 what was Porter Wagoner's first hit record?

A. "A Satisfied Mind."

———◆———

Q. Where was actress Kathleen Turner born on June 19, 1954?

A. Springfield.

———◆———

Q. The majority of Branson's music theaters are situated along what highway?

A. Missouri 76.

Q. The theme and background music for such television series as "Six Million Dollar Man," "Longstreet," and "Matt Lincoln" were the work of what St. Louis native?

A. Oliver Edward Nelson.

———◆———

Q. What television game show host attended Drury College in Springfield?

A. Bob Barker.

———◆———

Q. *Gallant Lady, Dark Angel* and *The Mark of Zorro* are all film credits of what Jefferson Citian?

A. Janet Beecher.

———◆———

Q. Jazz trumpter Joseph Lewis ("Joe") Thomas was born in what Missouri town on July 24, 1909?

A. Webster Groves.

———◆———

Q. What actress from Kirksville received three Academy Award nominations during her screen career?

A. Geraldine Page.

———◆———

Q. When was actor Vincent Price born in St. Louis?

A. May 27, 1911.

———◆———

Q. In 1938 what Warrensburg-born actor took over the title role in the popular Charlie Chan movie series?

A. Sidney Toler.

Q. St. Louis native Redd Foxx appeared in what television comedy series from January 14, 1972, to September 2, 1977?

A. "Sanford and Son."

———◆———

Q. What host of the television nature series "Wild Kingdom" was born in Carthage in 1905?

A. Marlin Perkins.

———◆———

Q. The motion pictures *Durango, Zero Hour, All the Young Men,* and *Jonathan Livingston Seagull* were directed by what native of Kansas City?

A. Hall Bartlett.

———◆———

Q. Missouri pianist Jess Alexandria Stacy played piano on the soundtrack of what 1975 motion picture?

A. *The Great Gatsby.*

———◆———

Q. What long-time member of the NBC orchestra for "The Tonight Show" was born in St. Louis in 1920?

A. Clark Terry.

———◆———

Q. *Dillinger, The Wind and the Lion, Conan the Barbarian,* and *Red Dawn* are all works of what St. Louis-born director?

A. John Milius.

———◆———

Q. Where was actor Steve McQueen born on March 24, 1930?

A. Slater.

Q. What Missourian served as host on the television game show "Win, Lose or Draw"?

A. Bert Convy.

———◆———

Q. In what community did comedienne/actress Phyllis Diller marry and raise her family?

A. Webster Groves.

———◆———

Q. Who composed music for such motion pictures as *What's New Pussycat?*, *Casino Royale*, *Butch Cassidy and the Sundance Kid*, *Lost Horizon*, and *Arthur?*

A. Burt Bacharach.

———◆———

Q. What was Missouri-born country performer Ferlin Husky's comic alter ego?

A. Simon Crum.

———◆———

Q. In what Missouri city was actor Irving Macon born in 1893?

A. St. Joseph.

———◆———

Q. What West Plains country comedian and fiddle player became well known for his two blackened front teeth and plaid suit?

A. Gilbert ("Speck") Rhodes.

———◆———

Q. For what role in the 1940 motion picture *The Grapes of Wrath* did Palmyra native Jane Darwell receive an Academy Award for best supporting actress?

A. Ma Joad.

Q. What pioneer boogie woogie piano player was born in Kansas City in 1904?

A. Pete Johnson.

———◆———

Q. Missouri-born Bob Cummings played what girl-crazy photographer in the 1950s television series "Love That Bob"?

A. Bob Collins.

———◆———

Q. What Dearborn native played the role of J. R.'s father in the television series "Dallas"?

A. Jim Davis.

———◆———

Q. Born in Hannibal in 1895, actor/musician Cliff Edwards was know by what stage name?

A. Ukelele Ike.

———◆———

Q. What vivacious screen actress of the late 1930s, 1940s, and 1950s was born Terry Ray in Kansas City on November 23, 1915?

A. Ellen Drew.

———◆———

Q. Where was actor Wallace Beery born on April 1, 1885?
A. Kansas City.

———◆———

Q. Dave Garroway, the first host of "The Today Show," attended what St. Louis High school?

A. University City High School.

Q. Actress Linda Blair gained international fame for her role in what 1973 thriller?

A. *The Exorcist.*

———◆———

Q. During what years was Missouri-born actress Jane Wyman married to Ronald Reagan?

A. 1940 to 1948.

———◆———

Q. In the classic 1954 movie *White Christmas,* what St. Louis native played General Waverly's housekeeper?

A. Mary Wickes.

———◆———

Q. Born in Missouri, Walter Cronkite was the chief news correspondent in what historic television series that debuted on February 1, 1953?

A. "You Are There."

———◆———

Q. What actress was born Shirley Schrift in St. Louis on August 18, 1922?

A. Shelley Winters.

———◆———

Q. Missouri-born country music singer Leona Williams married what country music performer in 1978?

A. Merle Haggard.

———◆———

Q. What musician from St. Joseph was one of the most influential figures in the development of the tenor saxophone in jazz?

A. Coleman Hawkins.

Q. In what city was actress Linda Blair born on January 22, 1959?

A. St. Louis.

———◆———

Q. Marshall-born musician Robert ("Bob") James arranged and conducted the music for what 1973 motion picture?

A. *Serpico.*

———◆———

Q. What Kansas Citian played Batman in the 1949 Columbia Pictures serial?

A. Robert Lowery.

———◆———

Q. What Missouri-born actress played opposite Gregory Peck in the 1951 movie *Captain Horatio Hornblower?*

A. Virginia Mayo.

———◆———

Q. Who was Kansas City-born Wallace Beery's older brother who appeared in such movies as *North of '36, East of Suez,* and *Noah's Ark?*

A. Noah Beery.

———◆———

Q. For what record did St. Louisians the Kendalls receive the CMA Single of the Year award in 1978?

A. "Heaven's Just a Sin Away."

———◆———

Q. What 1973 movie featured several St. Joseph locations?

A. *Paper Moon.*

Q. Missouri native Ginger Rogers won an Academy Award for best actress in what 1940 motion picture?

A. *Kitty Foyle.*

———————◆———————

Q. Rock 'n' roll great Chuck Berry attended what St. Louis high school?

A. Sumner High School.

———————◆———————

Q. Both the 1940 and 1964 film versions of Harold Bell Wright's novel *Shepherd of the Hills* were shot in and around what southern Missouri town?

A. Branson.

———————◆———————

Q. What restored 1929 St. Louis movie palace now serves as a venue for plays and concerts?

A. Fox Theatre.

———————◆———————

Q. Actor Lynne Overman, whose movie credits included *Little Miss Marker, Big Broadcast of 1938,* and *Northwest Mounted Police,* was born in what town?

A. Maryville.

———————◆———————

Q. What Missourian teamed with Bill Anderson in 1967 to record the number-one country hit "For Loving You"?

A. Jan Howard.

———————◆———————

Q. Joplin native Pauline Starke made her screen debut in what 1916 D. W. Griffith movie?

A. *Intolerance.*

Q. What was the theme song of the country music television series "Ozark Jubilee"?

A. "Sugarfoot Rag."

Q. Where was actor James Franciscus born on January 31, 1934?

A. Clayton.

Q. What popular pinup girl of World War II was born in St. Louis in 1916?

A. Betty Grable.

Q. Actress Tammy Grimes attended what institution of higher learning in Columbia?

A. Stephens College.

Q. What actor from St. Louis has appeared in such movies as *The Great White Hope, Shaft, The Iceman Cometh, Rollerball, Ragtime,* and *Firestarter?*

A. Moses Gunn.

Q. In what city was actress Jean Harlow born on March 3, 1911?

A. Kansas City.

Q. What 1961 movie starring Keir Dullea and Don Murray was shot in Jefferson City and St. Louis?

A. *The Hoodlum Priest.*

Q. The country-rock band Ozark Mountain Daredevils was organized in what city?

A. Springfield.

◆

Q. In what two movies did Missouri-born country comedian Whitey Ford appear?

A. *Country Farm* and *Country Music on Broadway.*

◆

Q. What St. Louis-born silent screen star appeared in the original film versions of *The Scarlet Letter* and *Ivanhoe?*

A. King Baggot.

◆

Q. For what 1931 movie did Missourian Wallace Beery win an Academy Award for best actor?

A. *The Champ.*

◆

Q. What is the actual name of Missouri-born actor John Ashley?

A. John Atchley.

◆

Q. What well-known talent scout of the 1920s and early 1930s was born in Kansas City in 1892?

A. Ralph Peer.

◆

Q. What accompanist and arranger for Tennessee Ernie Ford taught music in the Hannibal school system during the 1930s?

A. Jack Fascinato.

Q. The long-running gospel music family group The Lesters work out of what Missouri city?

A. St. Louis.

Q. What Missourian received an Academy Award for best director of photography for his work in the 1946 motion picture *The Yearling?*

A. Arthur Arling.

Q. The "locked hands" piano style was popularized by what multi-instrumentalist from St. Louis?

A. Milton ("Milt") Buckner.

Q. What comedian was born John Elroy Sanford in St. Louis on December 9, 1922?

A. Redd Foxx.

Q. In what Missouri community did Walt Disney spend most of his childhood?

A. Marceline.

Q. Jamesport native Martha Scott played what role in the 1940 movie version of *Our Town?*

A. Emily Webb.

Q. What St. Louis native appeared in such movies as *Babbitt, It's a Wonderful Life,* and *The Birds and the Bees?*

A. Mary Lou Treen.

Q. In what year did "The Porter Wagoner Show" start its long television run?

A. 1960.

---◆---

Q. What St. Louis-born actress married Neil Simon?

A. Marsha Mason.

---◆---

Q. Ben Moses, who co-produced the motion picture *Good Morning Vietnam,* attended what Missouri college?

A. Washington University.

---◆---

Q. Television producer/writer Linda Bloodworth-Thomason, who co-founded Mozark Productions in 1983, was born in what town?

A. Poplar Bluff.

---◆---

Q. In addition to his many stage and television credits, what St. Louis actor appeared in the motion pictures *Hurry Sundown* and *Hour of the Gun?*

A. Frank Converse.

---◆---

Q. What country music singer/songwriter was born in Flat River on December 3, 1927?

A. Ferlin Husky.

---◆---

Q. St. Louis-born musician Charles E. Kynard scored the music for what 1969 movie?

A. *Midtown Madness.*

Q. What was Helen Cornelius's first release for RCA Records in 1975?

A. "We Still Love Songs in Missouri."

———◆———

Q. Where was actor/director Bob Cummings born on June 10, 1908?

A. Joplin.

———◆———

Q. What Missourian made his screen debut in the 1958 sci-fi thriller *The Blob?*

A. Steve McQueen.

———◆———

Q. After the Civil War, what performing troop conducted a belated funeral service in Richmond for Confederate guerrilla leader Capt. Bill Anderson?

A. The Cole Younger Circus and Wild West Show.

———◆———

Q. What 1970 movie starring Michael Douglas was filmed in part in the Excelsior Springs area?

A. *Adam at 6 A.M.*

———◆———

Q. Where was music performer Billy Swan born on May 12, 1942?

A. Cape Girardeau.

———◆———

Q. What Missourian played opposite Rudolph Valentino in *The Sheik* and Lon Chaney in *The Hunchback of Notre Dame?*

A. Patsy Ruth Miller.

Q. In what year was Kansas City's historic Folly Theater constructed?

A. 1900.

━━━━◆━━━━

Q. What St. Louis attraction features a demonstration on the construction of marionettes and musical puppet presentations?

A. Bob Kramer Marionettes.

━━━━◆━━━━

Q. Pattonsburg was the hometown of what star of the Columbia Pictures serial *Great Adventures of Wild Bill Hickok?*

A. William Elliott.

━━━━◆━━━━

Q. What character actor and regular on the "Dobie Gillis" television series was born in St. Louis in 1904?

A. Frank Faylen.

━━━━◆━━━━

Q. Actress Ginger Rogers was born in what city on July 16, 1911?

A. Independence.

━━━━◆━━━━

Q. What is actress Mary Frann's real name?

A. Frances Luecke.

━━━━◆━━━━

Q. *The Maltese Falcon, The Treasure of the Sierra Madre,* and *The Man Who Would Be King* are among the many movies directed by what Nevada native?

A. John Huston.

Q. What 1974 independent road film was shot primarily in St. Joseph?

A. *Supervan.*

———◆———

Q. *Cashbox* magazine voted what St. Louis duo Most Promising Vocal Group of 1968–69?

A. Compton Brothers.

———◆———

Q. What host of the television game show "Name That Tune" attended the University of Missouri, Columbia?

A. Tom Kennedy.

———◆———

Q. One episode of what long-running television canine series was filmed in Meramec Caverns?

A. "Lassie."

———◆———

Q. Nationally syndicated radio talk show host Rush Limbaugh graduated in 1969 from what Missouri high school?

A. Cape Girardeau Central High School.

———◆———

Q. Humansville native Edgar Buchanan played what role in the television series "Petticoat Junction"?

A. Uncle Joe.

———◆———

Q. What award-winning gospel tenor was born in Salem on October 3, 1958?

A. Garry ("Squeeky") Sheppard.

Q. In 1938, what movie starring Tyrone Power and Henry Fonda was shot in and around Pineville?

A. *Jesse James.*

———◆———

Q. What actress, who has appeared in such movies as *Tender Mercies, Silkwood, Flash Point,* and *Crimes of the Heart,* attended Southwest Missouri State University?

A. Tess Harper.

———◆———

Q. Kansas City locations were used in the filming of what 1972 movie starring Lee Marvin and Gene Hackman?

A. *Prime Cut.*

———◆———

Q. During what years did "The Wilburn Brothers Show" run on television?

A. 1963–1969.

———◆———

Q. St. Louisian Betty Thomas played a tough lady cop in what television series?

A. "Hill Street Blues."

———◆———

Q. What actress was born Sarah Jane Fulks in St. Joseph on January 4, 1914?

A. Jane Wyman.

———◆———

Q. Bluegrass musicians Doug and Rodney Dillard were born in what town?

A. Salem.

Q. What actor known for his television roles in "Gunsmoke," "Kentucky Jones," and "McCloud" was born in Joplin in 1924?

A. Dennis Weaver.

Q. What motion picture tribute to the Father of Rock 'n' Roll was shot entirely in the St. Louis area?

A. *Hail, Hail, Rock 'n' Roll: The Chuck Berry Story.*

Q. In 1947 what television station became the first to broadcast commercially in the state?

A. KSD-TV, St. Louis.

Q. For what screenplay did St. Louisian Sally Benson receive an Academy Award nomination in 1946?

A. *Anna and the King of Siam.*

Q. What 1991 film based on two Evan S. Connell novels and starring Paul Newman and Joanne Woodward was filmed in Kansas City?

A. *Mr. and Mrs. Bridge.*

Q. The bestselling novel *King's Row* by Fulton-born Henry Bellamann was made into a movie starring what actor?

A. Ronald Reagan.

Q. What Kansas City animator was an early partner of and collaborator with Walt Disney?

A. Ub Iwerks.

Q. What entrepreneur founded Kansas City's huge greeting card company which consistently sponsors award-winning dramatic productions on television?

A. Joyce Hall (of Hallmark).

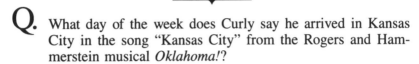

Q. What day of the week does Curly say he arrived in Kansas City in the song "Kansas City" from the Rogers and Hammerstein musical *Oklahoma!*?

A. Friday.

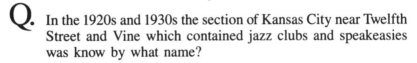

Q. In the 1920s and 1930s the section of Kansas City near Twelfth Street and Vine which contained jazz clubs and speakeasies was know by what name?

A. Little New York.

Q. What actor was highly successful in his one-man show *Mark Twain Tonight?*

A. Hal Holbrook.

Q. What bandleader-composer wrote "St. Louis Blues" in 1914?

A. W. C. Handy.

Q. What Columbia beauty was Miss America for 1990?

A. Debbye Turner.

Q. Ed Asner of "The Mary Tyler Moore Show" was born in what city on November 15, 1929?

A. Kansas City.

HISTORY

C H A P T E R   T H R E E

Q. In 1826 the Missouri legislature abolished what three forms of punishment for convicted criminals?

A. Whipping post, pillory, and stocks.

◆

Q. Though a white man, what early Bridgeton settler was the chief of a Shawnee tribe?

A. Lewis Rogers.

◆

Q. In what year did Missouri hold its first presidential primary?

A. 1988.

◆

Q. What future Missouri state senator and U.S. district attorney was wounded while a member of the Lewis and Clark Expedition?

A. George ("Peg-leg") Shannon.

◆

Q. The 1849 cholera epidemic killed how many St. Louis residents?

A. 4,060.

Q. When it was incorporated in 1919, what Cassville-area railroad had the distinction of being the shortest regulation, broad-gauged railroad in the nation?

A. Cassville and Exeter Railroad.

———◆———

Q. What transcontinental mail service was inaugurated on April 3, 1860, from St. Joseph?

A. The pony express.

———◆———

Q. North Carolinian James Jones erected what tavern on the Boon's Lick Trail in 1834?

A. Cross Keys Tavern.

———◆———

Q. Who opened the Danville Female Academy in 1856?

A. Prof. James H. Robinson.

———◆———

Q. What University of Missouri graduate was America's richest man at the time of his death of 1992?

A. Sam Walton.

———◆———

Q. In 1870, what two steamboats drew national attention with their race from New Orleans to St. Louis?

A. The *Natchez* and the *Robert E. Lee*.

———◆———

Q. Who was the founder of Springfield?

A. John Polk Campbell.

Q. What explorer passed the mouth of the Missouri River on February 14, 1682?

A. Robert Cavelier, Sieur de La Salle.

———◆———

Q. The 1839 border dispute between Missouri and Iowa was given what name?

A. Honey War.

———◆———

Q. What former business partner of naturalist/painter John James Audubon became the first mayor of Ste. Genevieve in 1827?

A. Ferdinand Rozier.

———◆———

Q. Who dedicated Kansas City's Liberty Memorial in 1926?

A. President Calvin Coolidge.

———◆———

Q. Around 1700, what group established the first white settlement in Missouri near the present site of St. Louis?

A. Jesuit missionaries (the Mission of St. Francis Xavier).

———◆———

Q. In 1849 what was the average daily number of steamboats using the wharf facilities at St. Joseph?

A. Twenty.

———◆———

Q. What new postal service was made available to many Missourians in 1896?

A. Rural mail delivery.

Q. Who shot and killed gambler Dave Tutt in a gunfight on the square in Springfield on July 21, 1865?

A. Charles Butler ("Wild Bill") Hickok.

———◆———

Q. Chartered at Ste. Genevieve in 1807, what was the first chapter of the Masonic order in Missouri?

A. Louisiana Lodge No. 109.

———◆———

Q. On December 20, 1847, what means of communication was established between St. Louis and the East?

A. The telegraph.

———◆———

Q. Completed at Kansas City in 1869, what was the first bridge to span the Missouri River?

A. Hannibal Bridge.

———◆———

Q. Central Methodist College in Fayette evolved out of what educational institution established in 1844 by Rev. William T. Lucky?

A. Howard High School.

———◆———

Q. What Missouri Civil War-era governor had three wives who were all daughters of Dr. John Sappington?

A. Claiborne Fox Jackson.

———◆———

Q. Who built the first house and operated the first store at Hannibal?

A. Moses D. Bates.

Q. What fortification was established by Sieur Etienne Veniard de Bourgmond in 1723 just west of the mouth of the Grand River?

A. Fort d'Orleans.

———◆———

Q. In 1821 what adventurer and trader left Franklin for New Mexico and in doing so blazed the Santa Fe Trail?

A. William Becknell.

———◆———

Q. What "town bully" was shot to death at Skidmore on July 10, 1981, in a vigilante-style daylight execution?

A. Ken Rex McElroy.

———◆———

Q. How many state constitutions has Missouri had?

A. Four (1820, 1865, 1875, 1945).

———◆———

Q. The last members of what Missouri native American tribe relocated to Kansas in 1837?

A. Osage.

———◆———

Q. Stretching forty-two miles, the nation's longest plank road was constructed between what two points in the early 1850s?

A. Ste. Genevieve and Iron Mountain.

———◆———

Q. What English engineer founded New London in 1814?

A. William Jamieson.

Q. When the Missouri National Guard was called into active duty in World War I, how many civilians were sworn into the Home Guard?

A. 10,000.

Q. To what position was Daniel Boone appointed in the Femme Osage district on July 11, 1800?

A. Syndic (judge).

Q. What Illinois engineer oversaw the construction of a covered bridge across the Salt River at Paris in 1857?

A. Robert Elliott.

Q. In April 1852, what side-wheel steamboat carrying 250 Mormons en route to Salt Lake City exploded near Lexington?

A. *Saluda*.

Q. What Ray County member of Missouri's first legislature later signed the Texas Declaration of Independence?

A. Ringtail Painter Palmer.

Q. At what cost was the first Jackson County courthouse erected at Independence in 1827?

A. $150.

Q. What late-nineteenth-century resident of Bowling Green served as Speaker of the House of Representatives for eight years?

A. James ("Champ") Beauchamp Clark.

Q. Vigilantes organized in Lincoln and Benton counties during the 1840s were know by what name?

A. Slickers.

Q. On March 3, 1862, what Union general laid siege to New Madrid?

A. Gen. Albert A. Pope.

Q. When it was constructed around 1800, what was the largest gristmill in the district of Cape Girardeau?

A. Bollinger Mill.

Q. In 1859 what Pike County resident flew 1,150 miles in a balloon from St. Louis to Henderson, New York?

A. John Wise.

Q. Who assumed command of Jefferson Barracks near Mehlville in 1855?

A. Robert E. Lee.

Q. In 1986 what was the per capita personal income in Missouri?

A. $13,657.

Q. Osceola was sacked and burned by what Kansas abolitionist and his men in September 1861?

A. Jim Lane.

Q. In what year was the city of St. Louis detached from St. Louis County and given an independent status equal to Missouri counties?

A. 1875.

Q. Following William Charles Quantrill's burning of Lawrence, Kansas, in August 1863, who issued Order No. 11, which basically evacuated all the residents of Jackson, Cass, Bates, and Vernon counties?

A. Gen. Thomas Ewing.

Q. How many bus lines were operating in Missouri in 1950?

A. 119.

Q. Because of the strong local sympathy for the Southern cause, by what nickname did the Missouri Valley heartland become known during the Civil War?

A. Little Dixie.

Q. What state agency was created in 1921 to construct and maintain the roads and highways of Missouri?

A. Missouri State Highway Commission.

Q. Although it was incorporated in 1847, the Hannibal and St. Joseph Railroad was completed in what year?

A. 1859.

Q. In 1910, where did Theodore Roosevelt become the first former U.S. president to fly in an airplane?

A. Kinloch Park, St. Louis.

Q. With what two colors did the Osage tribe paint their bodies for feast days?

A. Black and vermillion.

———◆———

Q. At what Kansas City facility was the nation's first sit-down strike at a manufacturing company carried out in 1936?

A. Leeds Chevrolet plant.

———◆———

Q. Who was the only man ever nominated by a national convention for vice president of the United States who resigned his candidacy?

A. Thomas F. Eagleton, U.S. senator from Missouri.

———◆———

Q. In 1833, who became the first settler on the site of present-day Warrensburg?

A. Martin Warren.

———◆———

Q. What woman was elected mayor of St. James in 1921?

A. Mayme H. Ousley.

———◆———

Q. What was the population of Columbia in 1830?

A. 600.

———◆———

Q. Who organized the Cape Girardeau Railway Corporation in 1880?

A. Louis Houck.

Q. Congressman Richard Parks Bland of Lebanon was given what nickname by his fellow congressmen for his fight for the unrestricted coinage of silver in the late 1800s?

A. Silver Dick.

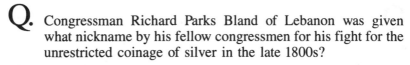

Q. The legislature chartered what Liberty institution of higher education on February 27, 1849?

A. William Jewell College.

Q. During the 1860s what percentage of Hannibal's population was black?

A. Approximately 40 percent.

Q. Who platted the site of Jefferson City in 1822?

A. Maj. Elias Bancroft.

Q. How many persons were killed on November 11, 1855, in the wreck of the first train to inaugurate the St. Louis to Jefferson City section of the Pacific Railroad?

A. Twenty-eight (with thirty injured).

Q. As a boy, what Indiana governor and vice president of the United States lived in La Grange?

A. Thomas Riley Marshall.

Q. In 1864, what combination orphanage and school was opened in Warrenton?

A. Western Orphan Asylum and Educational Institute.

Q. In what year did Spaniards erect a fort on the Mississippi River at Portage Des Sioux?

A. 1799.

————◆————

Q. What Gothic Revival-style church building was constructed at St. Peters in 1874?

A. All Saints Church.

————◆————

Q. On October 14, 1864, what Confederate guerrilla band burned Danville?

A. Anderson's Raiders.

————◆————

Q. Who established a ferry at Rocheport on the Missouri River in 1819?

A. John Gray.

————◆————

Q. In 1833, the legislature authorized what type of fund raiser to generate money for the construction of a mile-long railroad from New Franklin to the Missouri River?

A. A lottery.

————◆————

Q. Out of Missouri's first fifteen governors, how many once lived in Howard County?

A. Eight.

————◆————

Q. What was the largest of the Boon's Lick forts during the War of 1812?

A. Cooper's Fort.

Q. St. Louis sheriff John Finn organized a posse of how many men to contend with the railroad strike of 1877?

A. 5,000.

———◆———

Q. Who was elected president of Missouri's constitutional convention in 1820?

A. David Barton.

———◆———

Q. During the Civil War the chief quartermaster for the U.S. Army spent how much money in St. Louis to secure supplies for Union troops?

A. $180 million.

———◆———

Q. In 1895–96 what town attempted to wrest the capital from Jefferson City?

A. Sedalia.

———◆———

Q. What was the weekly rate charged for a room at the City Hotel and Livery in Noel in 1909?

A. Six dollars.

———◆———

Q. In what year was the Kansas City Municipal Airport replaced by the Kansas City International Airport?

A. 1972.

———◆———

Q. Approximately how many Union prisoners did Confederate general Sterling Price and his troops capture at the battle of Lexington?

A. 3,000.

Q. What Presbyterian minister was the first settler of Sweet Springs in 1826?

A. John Yantes.

———◆———

Q. After ten years in office, who resigned as state treasurer in 1861 rather than swear allegiance to the Union?

A. Judge Alfred W. Morrison.

———◆———

Q. Between what two St. Louis parks was the nation's first airmail flown on October 4, 1911?

A. Kinloch Park to Fairgrounds Park.

———◆———

Q. After many years of profitable operation, what revenue-generating program was discontinued by the legislature in 1877?

A. The Missouri State Lottery.

———◆———

Q. What noted Western scout, hunter, and soldier spent his childhood in the Boon's Lick area?

A. Kit Carson.

———◆———

Q. At the bidding of Emperor Maximilian, what noted Missouri political and military leader attempted to establish a colony of ex-Confederate soldiers near Cordova, Mexico?

A. Gen. Sterling Price.

———◆———

Q. What financial institution was organized in Southwest City on January 1, 1908?

A. Peoples Bank.

Q. Whose Boonville cabin served as the first courthouse for Howard County in 1816?

A. Hannah Cole's.

———◆———

Q. Dating back to 1821, what Florissant structure is believed to be the oldest Catholic church between the Mississippi River and the Rocky Mountains?

A. Old St. Ferdinand Shrine.

———◆———

Q. The failure of what St. Louis banking house on October 6, 1857, set in motion a statewide economic panic?

A. James H. Lucas and Company.

———◆———

Q. In 1838 who became the first settler in the area of present-day Joplin?

A. J. C. Cox.

———◆———

Q. What military educational institution was founded at Lexington in 1880?

A. Wentworth Military Academy.

———◆———

Q. At St. Louis on June 21, 1923, who became the first U.S. president to give a public address via radio?

A. Warren G. Harding.

———◆———

Q. What town hosted the Missouri legislature from 1821 to 1826?

A. St. Charles.

Q. In 1843 and again in 1844, followers of what religious sect ascended Lover's Leap at Hannibal only to be disappointed when they were not caught up into heaven?

A. Millerites.

———◆———

Q. How many families lived in Jefferson City in 1823?

A. Two.

———◆———

Q. In the 1950s what St. Louisians became the first blind couple in the nation to legally adopt a child?

A. Jim and Ethel Lee.

———◆———

Q. What was outlaw Belle Starr's maiden name?

A. Belle Shirley.

———◆———

Q. The Lutheran Church-Missouri Synod, the second-largest group of that denomination, was founded in what year?

A. 1847.

———◆———

Q. Where was the world's first railroad mail-car constructed in 1862?

A. Hannibal.

———◆———

Q. At what Fulton educational facility did Sir Winston Churchill make his famous Iron Curtain speech in 1946?

A. Westminster College.

Q. How many Missourians, both military and civilian, were killed during the Civil War?

A. Approximately 27,000.

———◆———

Q. What motto was adopted by the Knights of Labor at a general assembly in St. Louis in January 1879?

A. All for One, One for All.

———◆———

Q. Leonard Woods, for whom the U.S. Army fort near Rolla was named, was the first to command what calvary regiment of Spanish-American War fame?

A. First U.S. Volunteer Cavalry, nicknamed Rough Riders.

———◆———

Q. What was the population of Missouri in 1840?

A. 383,702.

———◆———

Q. Under terms of the Missouri Compromise, what state was admitted to the Union as a free state when Missouri was admitted as a slave state?

A. Maine.

———◆———

Q. What plan for the creation of a large military force, authored by Missourian Enoch Herbert Crowder, was adopted by the federal government on May 18, 1917?

A. The Selective Service Act.

———◆———

Q. By what name were some 180 French communists called who came with utopian Etienne Cabet to St. Louis in 1856?

A. Icarians.

Q. In 1912, the U.S. Congress appropriated how much money to improve the Missouri River from its mouth to Kansas City?

A. $20 million.

Q. In 1823, what two native American tribes relinquished the last of their land holdings in Missouri?

A. The Sauk and the Fox.

Q. How many automobiles were registered in Missouri in 1901?

A. 16,387.

Q. What was the name of the airplane in which Charles A. Lindbergh became the first person to fly solo across the Atlantic Ocean in 1927?

A. *Spirit of St. Louis.*

Q. The Boot Heel section was included in Missouri's final boundaries through the vigorous campaigning of what early settler from the Caruthersville area?

A. John Hardeman Walker.

Q. What was the middle name of Missouri-born outlaw Jesse James?

A. Woodson.

Q. When it went on the air in St. Louis on April 26, 1921, what were the call letters of Missouri's first radio station?

A. 9YK.

Q. Following the Civil War, what slave-born educator opened the first school for blacks in the state?

A. James Milton Turner.

———————◆———————

Q. In 1803 the United States paid Napoleon approximately how much per acre for the Louisiana Territory, including present-day Missouri?

A. Less than three cents (828,000 square miles for $15 million).

———————◆———————

Q. How many Confederate soldiers were executed on October 18, 1862, at the Palmyra fairgrounds by order of Col. John McNeil?

A. Ten.

———————◆———————

Q. What ethnic group founded Hawk Point in Lincoln County in the early 1840s?

A. Bohemians.

———————◆———————

Q. Who were Missouri's first two U.S. senators?

A. David Barton and Thomas Hart Benton.

———————◆———————

Q. In 1881 St. Louis street car conductors and drivers went on strike to get their workday reduced to what length?

A. Twelve hours.

———————◆———————

Q. How many slaves were in Missouri in 1860?

A. 114,930.

Q. What agency was formed on April 24, 1917, which served as the supreme authority within the state for twenty-one months during the national crisis caused by World War I?

A. Missouri Council of Defense.

———◆———

Q. Constructed at Hannibal in 1865, the first steam locomotive to be built west of the Mississippi River was given what name?

A. General Grant.

———◆———

Q. What labor organization was formed in St. Louis in 1861?

A. American Miners' Association.

———◆———

Q. In 1939 what LaForge resident organized more than 1,000 tenant farmers to camp along U.S. 61 in an attempt to bring national attention to the plight of sharecroppers?

A. Rev. Owen H. Whitefield.

———◆———

Q. What Missouri Civil War battle fought on October 23, 1864, was called the "Gettysburg of the West"?

A. Battle of Westport.

———◆———

Q. The enactment of what 1921 legislation ushered in modern systematic highway construction and maintenance in the state?

A. Centennial Road Law.

———◆———

Q. What was the first railroad to reach Kansas City in 1865?

A. The Pacific Railroad.

Q. During its peak in the mid-1800s, the firm of Russell, Majors, and Waddell had how many wagons transporting goods from St. Louis to points west?

A. 4,000.

Q. Who was the first mayor of Columbia?

A. Col. Richard Gentry.

Q. What was the construction cost of Missouri's present-day capitol when it was completed in 1917?

A. $4,125,000.

Q. Who was nominated for the presidency of the United States at the Democratic National Convention held in St. Louis in 1876?

A. Samuel J. Tilden.

Q. In 1820, what Osage leader headed a delegation to Washington, D.C., to secure the establishment of a mission school in what is present-day Bath County?

A. Chief White Hairs.

Q. What Ste. Genevieve house, built in 1770, now serves as a historical museum?

A. Amoureaux House.

Q. What governor, who served from 1832 to 1836, is credited with having founded the public school system in Missouri?

A. Daniel Dunklin.

Q. Who launched the Missouri Farmers Association in Columbia in 1914?

A. William Hirth.

———◆———

Q. During the Panic of 1837, wages in Missouri dropped by what percentage?

A. 50 to 75 percent.

———◆———

Q. Built in Monroe County in 1870, what is the last surviving covered bridge in the state constructed with a "Burr-arch" truss?

A. Union Covered Bridge.

———◆———

Q. During what years did Missourian Harry S Truman serve as president of the United States?

A. 1945–1953.

———◆———

Q. With what unit of the Missouri National Guard did Charles A. Lindbergh serve?

A. 110th Observation Squadron.

———◆———

Q. In what year did Adolphus Busch purchase a junior partnership in the St. Louis brewery of his father-in-law, Eberhard Anheuser?

A. 1865.

———◆———

Q. Maj. Gen. Sterling Price, who led the Missouri Militia during the Civil War, was known by what nickname?

A. Old Pop.

Q. What national aviation event was held at St. Louis in 1907?

A. Great American Air Meet.

———◆———

Q. In 1939 the legislature authorized state control over what municipality's police department because of corruption within that city's government?

A. Kansas City.

———◆———

Q. At the outbreak of the War of 1812, how many federal troops were stationed in the entire Missouri Territory?

A. 178.

———◆———

Q. What Missouri governor ordered the state milita in 1838 either to exterminate the Mormons or to drive them from the state?

A. Lilburn W. Boggs.

———◆———

Q. Who founded the utopian settlements of Friendship Community, Mutual Aid Community, and Altruist Community in Missouri in the 1870s and 1880s?

A. Alcander Longley.

———◆———

Q. How many foreign nations were represented at the St. Louis World's Fair in 1904 (Louisiana Purchase Exposition)?

A. Sixty-two.

———◆———

Q. Who was acquitted of train robbery charges at the courthouse in Gallatin in 1882?

A. Frank James, brother of Jesse James.

Q. Lexington was settled around what Missouri River enterprise?

A. William Jack's ferry.

Q. In what year was the Missouri Highway Patrol established?

A. 1931.

Q. Who organized the first regiment of Missouri Mounted Volunteers to fight in the Mexican War?

A. Alexander William Doniphan.

Q. From 1897 to 1905, who headed a group of socialists who conducted a cooperative experiment in business and education at Trenton?

A. Walter Vrooman.

Q. In 1857 what was the last recorded steamboat to make a trip on the Grand River?

A. The *Bonita*.

Q. Dedicated on July 4, 1874, and spanning the Mississippi River at St. Louis, what was the world's first steel-truss bridge?

A. Eads Bridge.

Q. Missouri provided how many men for service in the Spanish-American War?

A. 8,109.

Q. Under an 1822 state law, free Missouri males ages 16 to 45 were required to assist in maintaining what public works in their local districts?

A. Roads.

———◆———

Q. What giant airship made an exhibition appearance at the Pulitzer Air Races at St. Louis in 1923?

A. *Shenandoah*.

———◆———

Q. Of the 2,555 Spanish land grant claims filed in Missouri with the U.S. government between 1814 and 1816, how many were not confirmed?

A. 801.

———◆———

Q. In what year did Missouri's first state house burn?

A. 1837.

———◆———

Q. What Missouri resident who moved into free territory owned the slave Dred Scott, the subject of the landmark ruling by the U.S. Supreme Court?

A. John Emerson.

———◆———

Q. Who is known as the Father of the University of Missouri?

A. Maj. James S. Rollins.

———◆———

Q. Where was Missouri's first city-owned light and power plant constructed in 1886?

A. Hannibal.

Q. What commander-in-chief of the U.S. Fleet from 1923 to 1925 was born in Hannibal in 1864?

A. Adm. Robert E. Coontz.

———◆———

Q. In 1869 what German immigrant defeated the Radical Republican candidate to win the U.S. Senate seat from Missouri?

A. Carl Schurz.

———◆———

Q. Constructed in 1808, what is believed to be the oldest brick home in St. Louis County?

A. Sappington House.

———◆———

Q. In what year were the first counties organized in Missouri under the auspices of the territorial government?

A. 1812.

———◆———

Q. What Missourian, while serving as president pro tem of the U.S. Senate, is believed by many technically to have been president of the United States for one day on March 4, 1849?

A. David Rice Atchison.

———◆———

Q. Who organized the first Baptist church west of the Mississippi River near Jackson on July 19, 1806?

A. Rev. David Green.

———◆———

Q. What internationally known retailer was born near Hamilton in 1875?

A. J. C. Penney.

Q. Who was the founder and first mayor of Sedalia?

A. Gen. George R. Smith.

———◆———

Q. The demand for zinc during World War I caused the population of Carterville to swell to what figure?

A. Approximately 12,000.

———◆———

Q. The slaves freed at the close of the Civil War represented what amount of investment loss to Missouri slaveholders?

A. Some $40 million.

———◆———

Q. Founded at Florissant on May 11, 1823, what was the nation's first native American boy's school?

A. St. Regis Seminary.

———◆———

Q. Where did Missouri's first state hospital for the treatment of the mentally ill open in 1849?

A. Fulton.

———◆———

Q. In 1830, what Old World royalty was the house guest of Ste. Genevieve resident Gen. John Bossier for three months?

A. King Otto of Greece.

———◆———

Q. What steamboat caught fire while docked at the St. Louis wharf on May 19, 1849, destroying several boats and fifteen blocks of businesses?

A. *White Cloud.*

Q. In 1948, what was the first dam in the state to be constructed by the U.S. Corps of Engineers?

A. Clearwater Dam.

Q. Under Missouri's first constitution, federal and state officials, ministers and priests could not be elected to what state office?

A. General Assembly.

Q. On what date did President James Monroe announce Missouri's statehood?

A. August 10, 1821.

Q. Who was the first federally appointed governor over the lands of the Louisiana Purchase?

A. Gen. James Wilkinson.

Q. During the 1920s what Democratic party boss gained control over Kansas City's government?

A. Thomas J. Pendergast.

Q. With what amount of capital was the Bank of St. Louis chartered on August 21, 1816?

A. $163,000.

Q. In what town was Missouri's Ordinance of Secession from the Union and the Act of Affiliation to the Confederate States signed in the fall of 1861?

A. Cassville.

Q. In 1853, what was the first co-educational college west of the Mississippi River to be granted a charter?

A. Christian University (now Culver-Stockton College).

———◆———

Q. What nickname was given by locals to the old Weaverville-Clarkton plank road of the 1800s?

A. Devil's Washboard.

———◆———

Q. Dr. Luther M. Kennett, for whom the town of Kennett is named, served St. Louis in what public office from 1849 to 1852?

A. Mayor.

———◆———

Q. During the 1830s and 1840s what southern Jefferson County resident was known as Queen Bevers, the Witch?

A. Prudence Bevis.

———◆———

Q. Serving from 1864 to 1868, who was Missouri's first Republican governor?

A. Thomas C. Fletcher.

———◆———

Q. What was the full name of Harry S Truman's bride on June 28, 1919?

A. Elizabeth ("Bess") Virginia Wallace.

———◆———

Q. In 1819, what Potosi resident conceived a plan, later carried out by his son, to establish a settlement in Texas?

A. Moses Austin.

Q. What was the amount paid to workers for a twelve-hour day in the Iron Mountain mines during the 1850s?

A. 90¢ to $1.10.

———◆———

Q. While stationed at Mexico in Audrain County in 1861, Ulysses S. Grant was promoted to what rank in the U.S. Army?

A. Brigadier general.

———◆———

Q. In 1930, what criminal built a lavish eighteen-room home, complete with an eighty-foot lookout tower, south of Yukon?

A. Harry Getchie (alias Harry Watson).

———◆———

Q. What was Missouri-born Calamity Jane's actual name?

A. Martha Canary.

———◆———

Q. In 1797, what was the standard rate charged by Capt. James Piggott to ferry a horse and rider across the Mississippi River at St. Louis?

A. Two dollars.

———◆———

Q. In 1923, what Missourian became the first U.S. ambassador to Cuba?

A. Enoch Herbert Crowder.

———◆———

Q. Where in the late 1870s was a factory opened in Buchanan County to manufacture wooden stirrups?

A. Agency.

Q. What Platte County resident captained the first wagon train on the Oregan Trail and later served as the first governor of the state of California?

A. Peter Hardeman Burnett.

———◆———

Q. How many plank roads were constructed in Missouri during the mid-1800s?

A. Seventeen.

———◆———

Q. In the 1890s what Carthage resident won a test case in the state supreme court allowing her to become the clerk of Jasper County, thus making her the first woman in the United States to hold elective office?

A. Annie Baxter.

———◆———

Q. Who explored the Osage River in 1806?

A. Zebulon M. Pike.

———◆———

Q. Where did the first U.S. Army recruiting office west of the Mississippi River open in July 1812?

A. Ste. Genevieve.

———◆———

Q. In what year was Camdenton founded?

A. 1929.

———◆———

Q. Occurring on the morning of August 10, 1861, what is considered to be the most significant Civil War battle fought in Missouri?

A. Battle of Wilson's Creek.

Q. What was the first east-west road in the state?

A. Boon's Lick Trail.

———◆———

Q. Maj. David McKee and Hugh Allen formed what organization in Clark County in 1854 to give protection against marauders?

A. Anti-Horse Thief Association.

———◆———

Q. Sam Hildebrand, Missouri murderer and outlaw during the 1800s, gave what name to his favorite gun?

A. Kill-Devil.

———◆———

Q. Gen. Nathaniel W. Watkins, who served several terms in the state legislature, was a half brother of what noted statesman?

A. Henry Clay.

———◆———

Q. What was the price of a buffalo robe in Missouri in 1804?

A. Six dollars.

———◆———

Q. Who received a government contract in 1850 to establish a monthly mail stage service from Independence to Salt Lake City, Utah?

A. Samuel H. Woodson.

———◆———

Q. What labor reform measure was passed by the state legislature in 1925?

A. Workmen's Compensation Law.

Q. Sporting a bow in the shape of a serpent's head, what steamboat plied the waters of the Missouri River to within seven miles of Council Bluffs, Iowa, in 1819?

A. *Western Engineer.*

———◆———

Q. In what year did the University of Kansas City become the University of Missouri–Kansas City?

A. 1963.

———◆———

Q. The Spanish established what military road between New Madrid and St. Louis in the early 1790s?

A. El Camino Real (The King's Highway).

———◆———

Q. What pledge of allegiance was instituted by the Radical Republicans in 1865 as a prerequisite to vote, hold office, preach, teach, or practice law in Missouri?

A. Test Oath.

———◆———

Q. What was Missouri-born J. C. Penney's full name?

A. James Cash Penney.

———◆———

Q. Between 1930 and 1933 the individual employment in Missouri dropped by what percentage?

A. 62 percent.

———◆———

Q. To whose 1899 speech is Missouri's nickname of the Show Me State usually traced?

A. U.S. Rep. Willard Duncan Vandiver.

ARTS & LITERATURE

C H A P T E R   F O U R

Q. Situated in Arrow Rock, what is Missouri's oldest professional summer repertory theater?

A. Lyceum Summer Theatre.

◆

Q. What Missouri-born playwright received the 1980 Pulitzer Prize for drama for his work *Talley's Folly?*

A. Lanford Wilson.

◆

Q. Who was the first recorded professional portraitist to reside in Missouri?

A. Francois M. Guyol (c. 1812).

◆

Q. Sculptor Frederick Cleveland Hibbard, known for such works as *Tom Sawyer and Huck Finn* and *Madonna of the Trail,* was born in what town?

A. Canton.

◆

Q. How many German-language newspapers were in publication in Missouri in 1880?

A. Nineteen.

Q. In 1928 what Kansas City native founded the pioneer country music publishing house Southern Music?

A. Ralph Peer.

———◆———

Q. What 1903 novel by Frank H. Sosey dealt with the Palmyra Massacre and other Civil War events?

A. *Robert Devoy.*

———◆———

Q. The title and lyrics of what frontier ballad make reference to an eastern Missouri county?

A. "Sweet Betsy from Pike."

———◆———

Q. In what town was editor and novelist Rupert Hughes born on January 31, 1872?

A. Lancaster.

———◆———

Q. What St. Louis painter of the mid-nineteenth century created such canvases as *Long Jake, The Indian Guide, The Voyageur,* and *The Trapper?*

A. Charles Deas.

———◆———

Q. In 1832, what Mormon newspaper began publication in Independence?

A. *The Morning and The Evening Star.*

———◆———

Q. What music journal edited by Laura Valworth Lull was published in Kansas City from 1913 to 1915?

A. *The Clef.*

Q. The Shepherd of the Hills Outdoor Theater is located in what Missouri town?

A. Branson.

———◆———

Q. In 1939, 20th Century-Fox commissioned what Missourian to design and paint the promotional poster art for their motion picture *Gone With the Wind?*

A. Thomas Hart Benton.

———◆———

Q. Who composed the popular song "St. Louis Rag"?

A. Tom Turpin.

———◆———

Q. What two artists accompanied the Long expedition up the Missouri River in 1819–20?

A. Titan Ramsay Peale and Samuel Seymour.

———◆———

Q. Who painted a portrait of the aged Daniel Boone in 1819?

A. Chester Harding.

———◆———

Q. What Benedictine monastery, established in Missouri in 1873, produces posters, greeting cards, and calendars?

A. Conception Abbey.

———◆———

Q. Where was playwright, author, poet, and lyricist Langston Hughes born on February 1, 1902?

A. Joplin.

Q. What illustrator born in St. Louis in 1883 produced works for such magazines as *Cosmopolitan, McClure's,* and *Munsey's?*

A. Lee F. Corney.

———◆———

Q. In what city may plays be enjoyed at the Ice House Theater?

A. St. Joseph.

———◆———

Q. What University of Missouri graduate wrote the famous 1929 headline "Wall Street Lays An Egg," heralding the stock market crash for *Variety?*

A. Claude Binyon.

———◆———

Q. In what town is the outdoor drama *The Life and Times of Jesse James* performed?

A. Kearney.

———◆———

Q. What leading nineteenth-century Missouri painter opened a studio in St. Louis in 1835?

A. George Caleb Bingham.

———◆———

Q. Who is the creator of the Precious Moments figurines?

A. Samuel J. Butcher.

———◆———

Q. What newspaper was established at Hannibal in 1837?

A. *Commercial Advertiser.*

Q. In the mid-1800s, who wrote the scandalous book *The Mysteries of St. Louis?*

A. Henry Boernstein.

———◆———

Q. What two ladies designed the Missouri state flag?

A. Marie Elizabeth Watkins Oliver and Mary Kochtitzky.

———◆———

Q. Berenice Morrison-Fuller's book *Plantation Life in Missouri* features what house constructed in Fayette in 1832 by Capt. William D. Swinney?

A. Sylvan Villa.

———◆———

Q. What award-winning Broadway musical was based on *The Adventures of Huckleberry Finn,* Missourian Mark Twain's classic novel?

A. *Big River.*

———◆———

Q. Who built and endowed a two-story library in Glasgow in 1866?

A. Col. Benjamin W. Lewis.

———◆———

Q. What long-time New York newspaper columnist of the early twentieth century was born in Plattsburg?

A. O. O. McIntyre.

———◆———

Q. In what year was the St. Louis Municipal Opera established?

A. 1919.

Q. The Ragtime Archives Collection is housed at what Sedalia educational facility?

A. State Fair Community College.

◆

Q. What pioneer Missouri physician published his medical book, *The Theory and Treatment of Fevers,* in 1844?

A. Dr. John Sappington.

◆

Q. Where was composer Carl Valentine Lachmund born in 1857?

A. Boonville.

◆

Q. What St. Louis journalist became nationally famous as a correspondent in the Franco-Prussian War?

A. Januarius Aloysius MacGahan.

◆

Q. Who created the sculpture works on the pediment of the Missouri capitol?

A. A. A. Weinman.

◆

Q. What award-winning dramatist, a dropout from the University of Missouri–Columbia, devoted his free time to honing his playwriting skills while working in a St. Louis shoe factory during the Great Depression?

A. Tennessee Williams.

◆

Q. In what work did novelist Jack Conroy vividly describe the decline of a Missouri coal mining community?

A. *The Disinherited.*

Q. Joseph Pulitzer merged what two St. Louis newspapers in 1878?

A. The *Post* and the *Dispatch*.

———◆———

Q. Though first published in 1914, what became the official Missouri state song in 1949?

A. "Missouri Waltz."

———◆———

Q. What strong representative of the second wave of abstract expressionist painters was born in St. Louis on October 18, 1906?

A. James Brooks.

———◆———

Q. In what town is located the historic Grundy County Jewett Norris Library?

A. Trenton.

———◆———

Q. John Breckenridge Ellis, long-time president of the Missouri Writer's Guild, was born near what town on February 11, 1870?

A. Hannibal.

———◆———

Q. In 1880, what Missouri native bought the San Francisco *Daily Examiner*, which he later gave to his son?

A. George Hearst, father of William Randolph Hearst.

———◆———

Q. What St. Louis-born screen writer produced the script for John Ford's 1946 western *My Darling Clementine?*

A. Winston Miller.

Q. Who established a zither factory in Washington in 1864?

A. Franz Schwarzer.

Q. In Harold Bell Wright's *The Calling of Dan Matthews*, Gordon's Mill was based on what actual Missouri gristmill?

A. Bennett's Mill.

Q. What Methodist preacher and educator founded the Canton Press in 1862?

A. Jesse W. Barrett.

Q. For what novel did Moberly writer Mrs. J. J. Gasparotti (Elizabeth Seifert) receive the $10,000 Dodd, Mead–Red Book prize in 1938?

A. *Young Doctor Galahad.*

Q. What organization was founded by newspaper editors meeting in St. Louis on May 17, 1867?

A. Missouri Press Association.

Q. Painter Virginia Carolyn Robinson was born in what Missouri town?

A. Maryville.

Q. What St. Louisian illustrated Sir Walter Scott's *Quentin Durwood?*

A. C. Bosseron Chambers.

Q. Missouri screenwriter William Rose received an Academy Award for what 1967 movie?

A. *Guess Who's Coming to Dinner.*

———◆———

Q. Pulitzer Prize-winning columnist and television correspondent Ron Power was born in what town?

A. Hannibal.

———◆———

Q. What actress made her professional debut at age eleven in the ballet and chorus of the St. Louis Opera?

A. Agnes Moorehead.

———◆———

Q. At age seventeen Thomas Hart Benton worked as a cartoonist for what Missouri newspaper?

A. Joplin *American.*

———◆———

Q. What painter born in St. Louis in 1886 created the award-winning canvas *Morning Shadows?*

A. Frank Swift Chase.

———◆———

Q. Who created the bronze statue of Thomas Jefferson in the Missouri capitol?

A. James E. Fraser.

———◆———

Q. In the late 1800s what commodity could be used to purchase tickets for a family to the Blackwell Opera House in Joplin?

A. A wheelbarrow load of lead or zinc ore.

Q. What long-time Powell resident composed the gospel music classic "I'll Fly Away"?

A. Albert E. Brumley.

———◆———

Q. In December 1938 what St. Louis daily experimented with sending facsimiles of its newspaper via shortwave radio?

A. The *Post-Dispatch*.

———◆———

Q. What Queen City writer, speaker, and educator was known as the "boy president" of the University of Wisconsin?

A. Glenn Frank.

———◆———

Q. Who designed the 600-seat New Theater in St. Louis in 1819?

A. Isaac H. Griffith.

———◆———

Q. What 1884 work by John Monteith is one of the earliest novels to be written about Missouri hill people?

A. *Parson Brooks*.

———◆———

Q. Poet and dramatist Zoë Adkins was born in what Missouri town in 1886?

A. Humansville.

———◆———

Q. Henry M. Stanley, who was sent to Africa by the New York *Herald* in 1869 to locate Scottish missionary Dr. David Livingstone, started his journalism career at what St. Louis newspaper?

A. The *Democrat*.

Q. Printed in 1808, what was the first book to be published in Missouri?

A. *The Laws of the Territory of Louisiana.*

———◆———

Q. What town was the prototype for Twin Mounds in E. W. Howe's *Story of a County Town?*

A. Bethany.

———◆———

Q. The Albrecht Art Museum is in what city?

A. St. Joseph.

———◆———

Q. What St. Louis-born poet rose to prominence in the early 1900s with such collections of works as *Helen of Troy and Other Poems, Rivers to the Sea, Love Songs,* and *Flame and Shadow?*

A. Sara Teasdale.

———◆———

Q. For what 1907 novel is Harold Bell Wright best remembered?

A. *Shepherd of the Hills.*

———◆———

Q. What luxurious 400-seat playhouse is situated in Kansas City's Crown Center complex?

A. American Heartland Theater.

———◆———

Q. Where was poet T. S. Eliot born in 1888?

A. St. Louis.

Q. What Maryville-born pioneer in public speaking and self-improvement wrote *How to Win Friends and Influence People*.

A. Dale Carnegie.

———◆———

Q. At what age did Walt Disney enroll at the Kansas City Art Institute?

A. Fourteen.

———◆———

Q. Published by the French Literary Society of St. Louis from 1854 to 1864, what was the most successful French-language newspaper in the state?

A. *Le Revue de l'Ouest*.

———◆———

Q. What 1935 novel by MacKinlay Kantor gave a vivid picture of fox hunting in Missouri?

A. *The Voice of Bugle Ann*.

———◆———

Q. In what city was painter, sculptor, illustrator, and writer Charles M. Russell born on March 19, 1864?

A. St. Louis.

———◆———

Q. In 1852, Mark Twain became the assistant editor of what Hannibal newspaper?

A. The *Journal*.

———◆———

Q. Who established the *Jeffersonian* newspaper at Jefferson City in 1826?

A. Calvin Gunn.

Q. What noted Missouri writer of the 1930s spent ten years in Pineville researching the speech and customs of hill people?

A. Vance Randolph.

Q. James Carroll-Beckwith, who became a prominent New York portrait painter, was born in what town in 1852?

A. Hannibal.

Q. What Rolla attraction is the home of professional summer stock theater?

A. Ozark Actors Theater.

Q. Where were all of Laura Ingalls Wilder's "Little House" books written?

A. Rocky Ridge Farm, Mansfield.

Q. What St. Louis-born painter founded the Taos, New Mexico, art colony around 1900?

A. Oscar E. Benninghaus.

Q. Established by Carl Daenzer in 1857, what became the most influential German-language newspaper in the state?

A. *Westiche Post.*

Q. What Sedalia music store owner helped bring Scott Joplin to national attention when he published Joplin's "Maple Leaf Rag" in 1899?

A. John Stark.

Q. Where does the Missouri Symphony Society present concerts in Columbia?

A. The Missouri Theater.

———◆———

Q. What is Kansas City's only year-round professional ballet organization?

A. State Ballet of Missouri.

———◆———

Q. In 1860, what art society and museum was established in St. Louis?

A. Western Academy of Art.

———◆———

Q. What motion picture screenwriter known for such scripts as *Spirit of St. Louis, In Harm's Way, Von Ryan's Express,* and *The Poseidon Adventure* was born in Hayti?

A. Wendell Mayes.

———◆———

Q. In 1844, what St. Louis theater scenery painter produced a panorama of the Mississippi River on a canvas strip said to have been four miles in length?

A. John Rowson Smith.

———◆———

Q. Situated in Boonville, what is the oldest theater west of the Allegheny Mountains?

A. Thespian Hall.

———◆———

Q. Born in St. Louis in 1894, George McManus originated what newspaper cartoon series?

A. "Maggie and Jiggs."

Q. What Missouri-born writer and artist penned *Trails Plowed Under?*

A. Charles M. Russell.

————◆————

Q. Established in 1819, what was the first weekly newspaper in Missouri west of St. Louis?

A. *Missouri Intelligencer and Boon's Lick Advertiser.*

————◆————

Q. What Kirksville lawyer wrote twenty-six novels in the late 1800s?

A. John R. Musick.

————◆————

Q. Where is the Missouri River Festival of the Arts held each summer?

A. Boonville.

————◆————

Q. The writings of what German official, a three-year resident of Warren County, were greatly responsible for the large influx of German emigrants into the state from 1830 to 1870?

A. Gottfried Duden.

————◆————

Q. Muralist Thomas Hart Benton was born in what town in 1889?

A. Neosho.

————◆————

Q. In 1917, Missouri poet Orrick Johns published what collection of his poems?

A. *Asphalt and Other Poems.*

Q. In *The Gilded Age,* Mark Twain based the character of Col. Mulberry Sellers upon what actual relative?

A. His uncle, James Quarles.

———◆———

Q. Who established the *Missouri Sentinel* at Paris in 1837?

A. Gen. Lucian J. Eastin.

———◆———

Q. What Kansas City art museum showcases the largest collection of Henry Moore bronzes in the nation?

A. Nelson-Atkins Museum of Art.

———◆———

Q. Noted Missouri monument sculptor Frederick C. Hibbard was born in what town?

A. Canton.

———◆———

Q. What two of the three original witnesses of the Book of Mormon are buried at Richmond?

A. David Whitmer and Oliver Cowdery.

———◆———

Q. During the Civil War, what uniquely named newspaper was published in Linn?

A. *Unterrified Democrat.*

———◆———

Q. What Missouri town was the prototype of Rose Wilder Lane's *The Old Home Town?*

A. Mansfield.

Arts & Literature

Q. In what year was Traveller's Community Theater established in Kirksville?

A. 1973.

———◆———

Q. How many acres is the Laumeier Sculpture Park in St. Louis?

A. Ninety-six.

———◆———

Q. What renowned architect designed the famed Wainwright Building in St. Louis in 1890–91, his first steel-framed sky-scraper?

A. Louis Sullivan.

———◆———

Q. What St. Louis facility maintains the world's largest collection of literary resources pertaining to Lutheranism in the United States?

A. Concordia Historical Institute.

———◆———

Q. Where is the Harold Bell Wright Theater and Museum?

A. Branson.

———◆———

Q. Who first established the humorous publication *Puck* in St. Louis around 1870, then moved publication to New York in 1879?

A. Joseph Keppler.

———◆———

Q. Established in 1836, what was Cape Girardeau's first newspaper?

A. *Patriot.*

Q. Eghert Van Alstyne, who composed the song "In the Shade of the Old Apple Tree," spent his early years in what town?

A. Hannibal.

———◆———

Q. What art complex is on the campus of Missouri Southern State College?

A. Spiva Art Center.

———◆———

Q. Founded in 1880, what is the nation's second oldest symphony orchestra?

A. The St. Louis Symphony Orchestra.

———◆———

Q. What Missourian wrote the novel *Meet Me in St. Louis?*

A. Salley Benson.

———◆———

Q. For what long-running feature did Paris newspaper columnist Tom Bodine receive national recognition?

A. "The Scrap Bag."

———◆———

Q. What creative art experience for children is sponsored by Hallmark Cards in Kansas City?

A. Kaleidoscope.

———◆———

Q. A bronze statue of what Roman goddess adorns the dome of the Missouri capitol?

A. Ceres.

Q. Where is the Blum Collection of Southwestern Indian Arts and Crafts on display?

A. Southeast Missouri State University Museum.

———◆———

Q. Who instituted free evening drawing classes at Washington University in 1875?

A. Halsey Cooley Ives.

———◆———

Q. The Community Council of the Performing Arts promotes stage productions at what Nevada facility?

A. Little Alley Theater.

———◆———

Q. Established by P. H. Murry at St. Louis in 1880, what was Missouri's first black newspaper?

A. *Advance.*

———◆———

Q. Where does the Sedalia Symphony perform?

A. Smith-Cotton Auditorium.

———◆———

Q. The autobiography *A Soldier's Story* relates the World War II experiences of what Clark-born general, who later became the first chairman of the Joint Chiefs of Staff?

A. Gen. Omar N. Bradley.

———◆———

Q. Who served as the editor of Liberty's *Tribune* newspaper from 1847 to 1888?

A. John Dougherty.

Q. What is the resident theatrical group of St. Joseph's historic Missouri Theater?

A. Robidoux Resident Theater.

———◆———

Q. Around 1900 *Richard Carvel* and *The Crisis* were both best-selling novels for what St. Louisian?

A. Winston Churchill.

———◆———

Q. On what date did Missouri's first newspaper, the *Missouri Gazette,* begin printing?

A. July 12, 1808.

———◆———

Q. What is Thomas Hart Benton's only autobiographical mural?

A. *Joplin at the Turn of Century, 1896–1906.*

———◆———

Q. Where was the first tax-supported library in the state established in 1889?

A. Hannibal.

———◆———

Q. Who designed Missouri's Executive Mansion?

A. George I. Barnett.

———◆———

Q. What actress was appointed as professor of drama at Stephens College in Columbia in 1937?

A. Maude Adams.

Q. In the early 1800s, army paymaster Alphonse Wetmore penned articles for the *Missouri Intellegencer* under what pseudonym?

A. Aurora Borealis.

———◆———

Q. What 7,800-seat amphitheater is in Kansas City's Swope Park?

A. Starlight Theater.

———◆———

Q. In 1820 how many newspapers were being published in Missouri?

A. Five.

———◆———

Q. What artist painted the sixteen original oil paintings illustrating scenes from *Tom Sawyer* and *Huckleberry Finn* which are on display at Mark Twain's home in Hannibal?

A. Norman Rockwell.

———◆———

Q. What is Missouri's largest community theater?

A. Springfield Little Theater.

———◆———

Q. To what former Missouri neighbor did Kit Carson dictate his autobiography around 1856?

A. Jesse B. Turley

———◆———

Q. What Hungarian immigrant who settled in St. Louis left in his will money for annual awards given for distinguished achievement in journalism, literature, drama, and music?

A. Joseph Pulitzer, founder and publisher of the St. Louis *Post-Dispatch*.

Q. At the request of the Missouri Board of Immigration, who wrote the 1867 pamphlet "The Resources of Missouri" to draw workers to the state?

A. Sylvester Waterhouse.

———◆———

Q. What restored 1909 theater is the home of the Springfield Regional Opera?

A. Landers Theater.

———◆———

Q. In 1873, who became the first West Plains resident to have a piano?

A. Cornelius Bolin.

———◆———

Q. What city is home to the Mid America Dance Company?

A. St. Louis.

———◆———

Q. In what year was the Houston *Herald* newspaper founded?

A. 1872.

———◆———

Q. What Kansas City art gallery is housed in the 1885 Webster School building?

A. Central Park Gallery.

———◆———

Q. Nelson Kneass, who set the poem "Alice Ben Bolt" to music, is buried in what town?

A. Chillicothe.

Q. Lecturer and author Dale Carnegie attended what Missouri college?

A. Warrensburg State Teachers College.

Q. Who established the *Nodaway Democrat* in 1864?

A. Albert P. Morehouse.

Q. What is the name of the town based on Hannibal which is the setting of Mark Twain's *The Adventures of Tom Sawyer?*

A. St. Petersburg.

Q. What was the boyhood home of journalist and author Edgar W. ("Ed") Howe, known as the Sage of Potato Hill?

A. Bethany.

Q. What Missouri author penned *Little Fiddler of the Ozarks* and *When the Light Burned Low?*

A. John Breckenridge Ellis.

Q. John Beauchamp Jones, who worked as a storekeeper in Franklin and Arrow Rock, published what frontier work in 1841?

A. *Wild Western Scenes.*

Q. What is the largest black performing arts organization in the state?

A. St. Louis Black Repertory Company.

Q. Where is the Margaret Harwell Art Museum?

A. Poplar Bluff.

Q. Who founded the *Missouri Herald* at Jackson in 1819?

A. Tubal E. Strange.

Q. The library of what Missouri college contains the Charles Haddon Spurgeon collection of Elizabethan and Puritan literature?

A. William Jewell College.

Q. In the 1890s, what Missourian produced such novels about Creole life as *Bayou Folk, A Night in Acadie,* and *The Awakening?*

A. Kate O'Flaherty Chopin.

Q. Gertrude Stein collaborated as librettist with what Kansas City-born Pulitzer Prize-winning composer on the operas *Four Saints in Three Acts* and *The Mother of Us All?*

A. Virgil Thomon.

Q. Edison Theater is on the campus of what St. Louis university?

A. Washington University.

Q. What 1836 work by Missourian Nathaniel Beverley Tusker was called by Edgar Allen Poe "the best American novel"?

A. *George Balcombe.*

Q. What prize-winning editorial cartoonist for the St. Louis *Post-Dispatch* from 1958 to 1962 is best known for his book *Up Front,* a collection of World War II cartoons?

A. William Henry ("Bill") Mauldin.

———◆———

Q. For what play did Zoë Akins receive a Pulitzer Prize in 1935?

A. *The Old Maid.*

———◆———

Q. Where in Monroe County was newspaper columnist Tom Bodine born in 1870?

A. Paris.

———◆———

Q. What Missourian invented a press and system whereby the visually impaired could set music in Braille?

A. Henry Robyn.

———◆———

Q. In 1821, who collected and had published *Missouri Harmony* or *A Choice Collection of Psalm Tunes, Hymns and Anthems?*

A. Allen D. Carden.

———◆———

Q. What popular St. Louis-born author and journalist wrote the poems "Little Boy Blue" and "Wynken, Blynken, and Nod"?

A. Eugene Field.

———◆———

Q. In what year did ragtime composer Scott Joplin move to Sedalia?

A. 1896.

Q. Featuring works by state, national, and international artists, the Ella Carothers Dunnegan Galley of Art is in what town?

A. Bolivar.

◆

Q. Who founded Missouri's first newspaper, the *Missouri Gazette?*

A. Joseph Charless.

◆

Q. In 1877, photography pioneer John H. Fitzgibbon founded what publications?

A. *St. Louis Photographer* and *Illustrated Monthly Journal.*

◆

Q. What St. Louis landmark is the main site of the annual Storytelling Festival?

A. The Gateway Arch.

◆

Q. By 1860 how many newspapers were being published in Missouri?

A. 154.

◆

Q. What 1894 Mark Twain novel was inspired by an 1830s Missouri murder trial?

A. *Pudd'nhead Wilson.*

◆

Q. What University of Missouri–Columbia professional school, founded in 1908, is the oldest of its kind in the world?

A. School of Journalism.

SPORTS & LEISURE

C H A P T E R F I V E

Q. On January 11, 1970, what team did the Kansas City Chiefs defeat, 23–7, in Super Bowl IV?

A. Minnesota Vikings.

Q. Bruce Campbell of the St. Louis Browns struck out how many times in 1932?

A. 104.

Q. What popular Missouri frontier sporting event consisted of a galloping horseman attempting to wring the greased neck of a goose suspended by its feet?

A. Goose pulling.

Q. Where was basketball great Bill Bradley born on July 28, 1943?

A. Crystal City.

Q. In what town does the Buffalo Days celebration feature a buffalo chip-throwing contest?

A. Greenfield.

Q. What baseball Hall of Famer was pitcher/manager for the St. Louis Cardinals in the 1904 and early 1905 season?

A. Kid Nichols.

———◆———

Q. How many home runs did Vincent Edward ("Bo") Jackson hit with the Kansas City Royals during the 1989 season?

A. Thirty-two.

———◆———

Q. Who was the top rusher in 1958, 1959, and 1960 for the University of Missouri football team?

A. Melvin G. West.

———◆———

Q. Harry E. ("Blackjack") Smith, the University of Southern California's star guard of the 1930s, was born in what Missouri town?

A. Russellville.

———◆———

Q. Where were the 1992 U.S. Fencing Association's Junior Olympic Championships held?

A. Kansas City.

———◆———

Q. Peaceful River and Hurricane Rapids are two of the features at what Branson water park?

A. White Water.

———◆———

Q. At what track near St. Charles were horses being raced as early as 1812?

A. Mamelle Track.

Q. What Missouri-born Basketball Hall of Fame member became a U.S. senator from New Jersey in 1979?

A. Bill Bradley.

———◆———

Q. How many hits did Stan Musial get during his long career with the Cardinals?

A. 3,630.

———◆———

Q. What years did St. Joseph native Emmett R. Stuber serve as head football coach at Southeast Missouri State University?

A. 1932 to 1946.

———◆———

Q. Before becoming a college coach, Gene Bartow coached basketball at high schools in what two Missouri towns?

A. Shelbina and St. Charles.

———◆———

Q. Where is the Ozark Mountain Anglers All Sport Show held each January?

A. Columbia.

———◆———

Q. Which Missouri college's athletic teams are called Vikings?

A. Missouri Valley College.

———◆———

Q. What competition of homemade, manpowered rafts is held on an arm of the Harry S Truman Reservoir between Roscoe and Osceola?

A. Great Raft Race.

Q. Walker Larry Dean Young set what American time record for the 30-mile walk at Columbia in 1971?

A. 4 hours, 11 minutes, 59.4 seconds.

———◆———

Q. What National Hockey League team is based in St. Louis?

A. St. Louis Blues.

———◆———

Q. In 1902, what two Missouri teams were participants in the Missouri Valley Baseball League?

A. Joplin and Jefferson City.

———◆———

Q. Where are the Show-Me-State Games held?

A. Columbia.

———◆———

Q. John ("Brick") Breeden, who coached basketball for forty-seven years at Montana State University, was born in what Missouri community?

A. Oyer.

———◆———

Q. What spring fishing competition takes place at Forsyth?

A. The White Bass Round-up.

———◆———

Q. In what year did St. Louis provide both the American League and the National League teams for the World Series?

A. 1944.

Q. Where may one scuba dive in a billion-gallon underground lake in the world's largest manmade cavern?

A. Bonne Terre Mine.

◆

Q. How old was pitching great Satchel Paige when he made his final appearance with the Kansas City A's in 1965?

A. Fifty-nine.

◆

Q. Where was catcher Walker Cooper born?

A. Atherton.

◆

Q. What attraction near Camdenton holds the record for the most underground weddings?

A. Bridal Cave.

◆

Q. With what team did James ("Cool Papa") Bell make his professional baseball debut in 1922?

A. St. Louis Stars.

◆

Q. Between 1899 and 1903, how many knockouts did Fulton native Aaron L. Brown score in twenty-seven fights?

A. Twenty-four.

◆

Q. The University of Oklahoma's Gomer Jones Award for best lineman went to what Malden native in 1972?

A. Derland Moore.

Q. Where is the finish line of the annual Missouri River Canoe/ Kayak Race and Fun Float?

A. Boonville's Missouri River Bridge.

◆

Q. In what year was the Missouri State Fair first held at Sedalia?

A. 1901.

◆

Q. What is the name of the St. Louis MISL soccer team?

A. St. Louis Storm.

◆

Q. With what team did Missouri-born baseball pioneer Clark Griffith sign his first pro contract in 1888?

A. Milwaukee.

◆

Q. What is the home playing field for the St. Louis Cardinals?

A. Busch Stadium.

◆

Q. The University of Kansas's 17,500-seat sports arena is named in honor of what Missourian?

A. Dr. Forrest Allen (Allen Field House).

◆

Q. What are the team colors of the University of Missouri?

A. Old gold and black.

Q. Who set a Lady Billiken basketball career scoring record between 1985 and 1990 with 1,479 points?

A. Julie Hacker.

———◆———

Q. Where was quarterback and coach James C. ("Jimmy") Conzelman born on March 6, 1898?

A. St. Louis.

———◆———

Q. The American Royal Livestock Horse Show and Rodeo, which dates from 1899, is held in what city?

A. Kansas City.

———◆———

Q. During what years did the American League Browns play in St. Louis?

A. 1902–1953.

———◆———

Q. St. Louis-born star first baseman Charlie Grimm was known by what nicknames?

A. Jolly Cholly.

———◆———

Q. During what years did Donald B. Faurot coach football at Northeast Missouri State University?

A. 1926–34.

———◆———

Q. According to the Missouri Division of Tourism, what is the most popular single attraction in the state?

A. The Gateway Arch in St. Louis.

Q. During what month is the annual month-long Fishing Derby held at the Lake of the Ozarks?

A. March.

◆

Q. What Kansas City Royal set the 1980 American League batting record with a .390 season average?

A. George Brett.

◆

Q. Sports teams at Missouri Southern State College are known by what names?

A. Lions and Lady Lions.

◆

Q. The 200-acre, Six Flags Over Mid-America theme park, featuring more than 100 rides, is situated near what town?

A. Eureka.

◆

Q. What is Springfield's most extravagant fireworks display?

A. Firefall.

◆

Q. In what year did St. Louis-born quarterback Clinton E. Frank receive the Maxwell Award and the Heisman Trophy?

A. 1937.

◆

Q. The Kansas City Royals play in what baseball league?

A. American League.

Q. What Cassville-born baseball player led the National League's third basemen in fielding in both 1967 and 1969?

A. Clete Boyer.

———◆———

Q. With what distance did Missourian Clarence Houser set a world's discus record on April 3, 1926?

A. 158 feet, 2 inches.

———◆———

Q. What water theme park is near Monroe City?

A. The Landing (at Mark Twain Lake).

———◆———

Q. What black Missouri baseball team played one of the first two professional night games on April 28, 1930 (the other taking place the same evening in Independence, Kansas, in the white leagues)?

A. Kansas City Monarchs.

———◆———

Q. What Easton native coached winning U.S. basketball teams in both the Tokyo and Mexico City Olympics?

A. Henry Iba.

———◆———

Q. At what facility is the Kansas City Jaycees Rodeo held?

A. Benjamin Ranch.

———◆———

Q. Wilbur ("Sparky") Stalcup had what win/lose record while coaching basketball at Northwest Missouri State University from 1934 to 1942?

A. 119–47.

Q. What Missouri school leads the NCAA in the most soccer championship wins?

A. Saint Louis University.

———◆———

Q. Harry W. Hughes, who served as head football coach at Colorado State University for thirty-one years, was born in what Missouri county in 1887?

A. DeKalb.

———◆———

Q. What German sausage-making competition is held each March in Hermann?

A. Wurstfest.

———◆———

Q. Kansas City is the home of what Major Indoor Soccer League team?

A. Comets.

———◆———

Q. Where is the Best Dam Run/Walk in America held each May?

A. Clarence Cannon Dam (Mark Twain Lake).

———◆———

Q. What maximum National League salary was Cy Young receiving when he moved with the Spiders franchise to St. Louis in 1899?

A. $2,400 per year.

———◆———

Q. Cardinals and A's pitcher Cloyd Boyer was born in what town?

A. Alba.

Q. What festival is held each September in Gainesville?

A. Hootin' an' Hollerin'.

———◆———

Q. What position did Jackie Robinson play with the Kansas City Monarchs?

A. Shortstop.

———◆———

Q. Phil ("Red") Murrell, star guard for both Moberley Junior College and Drake University, was born in what town in 1933?

A. Purdi.

———◆———

Q. What Kansas City Chief kicked a forty-eight-yard field goal during Super Bowl IV?

A. Jan Stenerud.

———◆———

Q. What Springfield retail facility is promoted as the World's Greatest Sporting Goods Store?

A. Bass Pro Shop's Outdoor World.

———◆———

Q. St. Louis-born pro quarterback and television football commentator Paul C. Christman was known by what two nicknames?

A. Pitchin' Paul and Merry Magician.

———◆———

Q. What is Yogi Berra's career batting average?

A. .285.

Q. The Hunt Midwest Enterprise underground facility at Kansas City is the site of what unique annual 10K underground run?

A. Groundhog Run.

———◆———

Q. What Yates native, best known as a collegiate coach and athletic director at the University of Southern California, played big-league baseball in the 1930s?

A. Jesse T. Hill.

———◆———

Q. Where is the National Bowling Hall of Fame and Museum?

A. St. Louis.

———◆———

Q. What 170-acre amusement park is situated northeast of Kansas City?

A. Worlds of Fun.

———◆———

Q. Where is the Lion Battlefield 5K run held?

A. Joplin.

———◆———

Q. What is the home playing field for the Missouri Southern State College football team?

A. Fred G. Hughes Stadium.

———◆———

Q. Pitcher Carl Hubbell, who played sixteen years with the New York Giants, was born in what town in 1903?

A. Carthage.

Q. The Northwest Missouri State University Bulldogs and Lady Bulldogs sport what team colors?

A. Purple and white.

———◆———

Q. What Saint Louis University basketball player went on to play for the St. Louis Hawks from 1960 to 1969?

A. Bob Ferry.

———◆———

Q. Who won the 1981 World Series?

A. St. Louis Cardinals.

———◆———

Q. What Missourian was the New York Yankees's first black player?

A. Elston Howard.

———◆———

Q. The University of Missouri is a member of what athletic conference?

A. Big Eight Conference.

———◆———

Q. What two years was Maryville represented in the MINK Baseball League?

A. 1910 and 1911.

———◆———

Q. In the Ozarks, what term was applied to the now-illegal catching of fish with bare hands?

A. Noodling.

Q. During the very hot summer of 1904 at the St. Louis World's Fair, Englishman Richard Blechynden was trying to increase usage of his company's product and served what beverage for the first time?

A. Iced tea.

———◆———

Q. In what year was Kansas Citian Casey Stengel inducted into the Baseball Hall of Fame?

A. 1966.

———◆———

Q. Where is the Miss Lake of the Ozarks beauty pageant held?

A. Osage Beach.

———◆———

Q. What are the names of Southwest Missouri State University's athletic teams?

A. Bears and Lady Bears.

———◆———

Q. Brutus Hamilton, who coached the 1952 U.S. Olympic track and field team, was born in what town?

A. Peculiar.

———◆———

Q. Pistol Pete was the nickname of what baseball slugger and Missouri native?

A. Harold Patrick ("Pete") Reiser.

———◆———

Q. In what month is the Sports Show held at Cape Girardeau?

A. February.

Q. What was Norm Stewart's first season as head basketball coach at the University of Missouri?

A. 1967–68.

————◆————

Q. The nineteenth-century St. Louis Browns of the American Association won how many pennants?

A. Four.

————◆————

Q. What facility on Highway 179 near Jefferson City offers equestrian rentals to riding enthusiasts?

A. Hidden Spring Stables.

————◆————

Q. Where was major-league catcher Johnny Kling born in 1875?

A. Kansas City.

————◆————

Q. What team did the University of Missouri defeat, 21–14, in the 1961 Orange Bowl?

A. Navy.

————◆————

Q. What Hannibal event features frog jumping, mud volleyball, and the National Fence Painting Contest?

A. National Tom Sawyer Days.

————◆————

Q. The St. Louis Cardinals football team was in the Eastern Division of which conference of the NFL?

A. National Conference.

Q. What are the team colors of Marshall's Missouri Valley College?

A. Purple and orange.

———◆———

Q. Where is the annual Missouri White Water Championship competition held?

A. Millstream Gardens State Park.

———◆———

Q. What two Missouri towns sponsor an annual turkey call and owl hooting contest?

A. Potosi and Steelville.

———◆———

Q. Where is the nation's third-largest St. Patrick's Day Parade held?

A. Kansas City.

———◆———

Q. What was the 1990 win/lose record for Northwest Missouri State University's football team?

A. 9–2.

———◆———

Q. Born in Green County in 1898, James ("Rabbit") Bradshaw played quarterback with what pro team in 1926?

A. Wilson Wildcats.

———◆———

Q. What eighteen-year veteran of the Brooklyn Dodgers was born in Hamilton in 1888?

A. Zack Wheat.

Q. Where is the Big Shot Family Action Park?

A. Linn Creek.

———◆———

Q. What two years did Cardinal pitcher Bob ("Gibby") Gibson suffer leg fractures during play?

A. 1962 and 1967.

———◆———

Q. In 1958, what St. Louis native won the vacant world welterweight title?

A. Virgil B. Akins.

———◆———

Q. What anglers' competition is held each April at Roaring River State Park?

A. Spring Trout Derby.

———◆———

Q. Which of the three professional baseball-playing Boyer brothers was born in Liberty?

A. Ken Boyer.

———◆———

Q. What Mexico attraction features a scuba diving lake, camping, hiking, and fishing?

A. The Hideout Aquatic Park.

———◆———

Q. Where was baseball great Yogi Berra born on May 12, 1925?

A. St. Louis.

Q. What licensed shooting preserve is situated north of Sumner?

A. Milford Gamebird Farm.

———————◆———————

Q. In 1991, what University of Missouri basketball player was a first-round draft pick by the Dallas Mavericks?

A. Doug Smith.

———————◆———————

Q. What Kansas Citian led the AFL in receiving for four of his first five years in the league?

A. Lionel Taylor.

———————◆———————

Q. Where was the first Missouri State Fair held?

A. Boonville.

———————◆———————

Q. In the summer of 1990, who became the director of athletics at Saint Louis University?

A. Debbie Yow.

———————◆———————

Q. When did the St. Louis Cardinals trade the colorful Dizzy Dean?

A. April 1938.

———————◆———————

Q. Where was baseball player, owner, and innovator Clark Griffith born in 1869?

A. Stringtown.

Q. During the 1989–90 season, what Billiken basketball player set a Saint Louis University game record by scoring forty-five points against Loyola?

A. Anthony Bonner.

———◆———

Q. What Kansas Citian, nicknamed Mount Washington, was the number-one draft pick of the San Diego Chargers in 1968?

A. Russell Washington.

———◆———

Q. Warsaw is the site of what three-day gamebird hunt and trap-shooting competition?

A. Missouri Invitational Celebrity Turkey Hunt.

———◆———

Q. What is the home court for the Missouri Valley College basketball team?

A. Burns Athletic Complex.

———◆———

Q. By what name are the University of Missouri–Kansas City sports teams known?

A. Kangaroos.

———◆———

Q. In the 1924 Paris Olympics, what Wennigin-born athlete won a gold medal in both discus and shotput?

A. Clarence Houser.

———◆———

Q. What nationally known country/pioneer theme park is situated near Branson?

A. Silver Dollar City.

Q. Missouri-born baseball legend Clark Griffith was known by what nickname?

A. The Old Fox.

———◆———

Q. What are the team colors of William Jewell University?

A. Cardinal red and black.

———◆———

Q. A black powder shoot and re-creations of Missouri life in the early 1800s are parts of what Old Mine's winter rendezvous?

A. Winter in La Vieille Mine.

———◆———

Q. What percentage of the University of Missouri's 1948 Gator Bowl team were native Missourians?

A. 100 percent.

———◆———

Q. On what date did Stan Musial get his first major league hit with the Cardinals?

A. September 17, 1941.

———◆———

Q. What University of Missouri Tiger captained the 1952 U.S. gold medal Olympic basketball team?

A. Dan Pippin.

———◆———

Q. Slugger Johnny Mize, who played with the St. Louis Cardinals from the spring of 1936 through the 1941 season, was known by what nickname?

A. Big Cat.

Q. What is the name of the million-gallon wave pool at Kansas City's Oceans of Fun water park?

A. Surf City.

———◆———

Q. In January 1988, the St. Louis Cardinals football team relocated to what city?

A. Phoenix, Arizona.

———◆———

Q. What are the team colors of the Southeast Missouri Indians and Otahakians?

A. Red and black.

———◆———

Q. New Point is the hometown of what 1969 number-one draft pick of the St. Louis Cardinals?

A. Roger R. Wehrli.

———◆———

Q. What chairlift ride affords a scenic view from the highest point on the Mississippi River, Lookout Point?

A. Clarksville Skyride.

———◆———

Q. Who was the St. Louisian who won a gold medal for the 110-meter hurdles at the 1924 Olympics?

A. Daniel Kinsey.

———◆———

Q. What baseball player from St. Louis became the National League's youngest-ever batting champion in 1941?

A. Pete Reiser.

Q. In what year did the St. Louis Cardinals adopt their name?

A. 1900.

————◆————

Q. What Missourian was honored with the Sullivan Award in 1965 as the nation's most outstanding amateur athlete?

A. Bill ("Dollar Bill") Bradley.

————◆————

Q. Saint Louis University is a member of what athletic conference?

A. Great Midwest Conference.

————◆————

Q. What St. Louis-born quarterback, nicknamed Rifle, played for the Rams, Redskins, Bears, and Steelers during the 1950s and 1960s?

A. Rudolph A. Bukich.

————◆————

Q. Who defeated the Kansas City Chiefs on January 15, 1967, in Super Bowl I?

A. Green Bay Packers.

————◆————

Q. What Scotland County native won a gold medal in the 110-meter hurdles at the 1932 Olympics in Los Angeles?

A. George Saling.

————◆————

Q. In what year did the Athletics establish themselves in Kansas City?

A. 1955.

Sports & Leisure

Q. What Stockton-born athlete received eleven collegiate letters in football, basketball, and baseball?

A. Emil ("Big Lis") Liston.

———◆———

Q. Where do the Kansas City Chiefs play their home games?

A. Arrowhead Stadium.

———◆———

Q. What is baseball legend Yogi Berra's full name?

A. Lawrence Peter Berra.

———◆———

Q. The sports teams of Missouri Baptist College are known by what names?

A. Spartans and Lady Spartans.

———◆———

Q. What was Bo Jackson's uniform number with the Kansas City Royals?

A. 16.

———◆———

Q. Twice AAU All-American Martin Nash was born in what town on February 16, 1920?

A. Holt.

———◆———

Q. What pitcher was the National League's MVP for the 1942 world champion Cardinals?

A. Mort Cooper.

Q. In the 1966 Sugar Bowl the Missouri Tigers defeated what team, 10–18?

A. Florida Gators.

———◆———

Q. What was Casey Stengel's actual name?

A. Charles Dillon Stengel.

———◆———

Q. Featuring an 18,000-square-foot wave pool, what water park is situated between Osage Beach and Camdenton?

A. Big Surf Waterpark.

———◆———

Q. What mid-March run is held at Jefferson City?

A. Luck of the Irish 5K Run and Walk.

———◆———

Q. The Miners and Lady Miners are the athletic teams of what Missouri university?

A. University of Missouri–Rolla.

———◆———

Q. What is the seating capacity of Memorial Stadium/Faurot Field in Columbia?

A. 62,000.

———◆———

Q. August J. ("Gus") Otto, pro linebacker during the 1960s and early 1970s, attended what St. Louis high school?

A. McBride High School.

Q. What was the nickname of the twentieth-century St. Louis Browns baseball team?

A. Brownies.

———◆———

Q. Helen Stephen, a double gold-winning sprinter at the 1936 Berlin Olympics, was born in what town?

A. Fulton.

———◆———

Q. What former University of Missouri coach is enshrined in the Basketball Hall of Fame?

A. Walter Meanwell.

———◆———

Q. Where is the Royalty Southwest Missouri Quarter Horse Show held each summer?

A. Carthage.

———◆———

Q. What baseball farm team of the St. Louis Cardinals is in Kentucky?

A. Louisville Redbirds.

———◆———

Q. Under what ring name did Missourian Aaron L. Brown box?

A. Dixie Kid.

———◆———

Q. What unique, laid-back event is held each February in Auxvasse?

A. Loafer's Week.

Q. Dr. Forest Allen, who served as the head basketball coach at the University of Kansas for thirty-nine years, was born in what Missouri town?

A. Jamesport.

✦

Q. At the St. Louis World's Fair, Americans were introduced to what two new foods?

A. Ice cream cones and hot dogs.

✦

Q. St. Louisian Elston Howard played in how many World Series?

A. Ten.

✦

Q. What Mt. Grove native originated football's split-T formation?

A. Donald B. Faurot.

✦

Q. George Sisler dazzled St. Louis Browns fans with what batting average during the 1922 season?

A. .420.

✦

Q. What national dart competition is held annually in the St. Louis area?

A. Blueberry Hill Dart Tournament.

✦

Q. In 1937, what Cardinal slugger won the National League's triple crown?

A. Joe ("Ducky") Medwick.

Q. What town is host to the Heart of the Ozarks Fair?

A. West Plains.

Q. Missourian Pete Reiser set a National League record by stealing how many home bases with the Dodgers in 1946?

A. Seven.

Q. Poke Salat Days, featuring a bed race, a 10K run, and a Little Mr. and Miss Poke is held in what community?

A. Ava.

Q. In 1985, who set a Billikens field hockey season record with sixty-two points scored?

A. Sandy Aden.

Q. What Charleston-born center was a member of the University of Kentucky's Fabulous Five during the 1940s?

A. Kenny Rollins.

Q. In what event did Independence-born walker Larry Dean Young receive bronze medals in both the 1968 and 1972 Olympics?

A. 50K walk.

Q. What St. Louisian played guard with the Phillips Oilers in 1939–40 and in 1943–45?

A. Fred Pralle.

Q. How many home runs did Ken Boyer hit with the Cardinals in 1960?

A. Thirty-two.

———◆———

Q. What town is host to the Great Pershing Balloon Derby?

A. Brookfield.

———◆———

Q. In 1973, the *Sporting News* honored what St. Louis native as NFL Executive of the Year?

A. James E. Finks.

———◆———

Q. What Forbes native was a long-time basketball coach at both Northwest Missouri State University and at the University of Missouri?

A. Wilbur ("Sparky") Stalcup.

———◆———

Q. Abroad what 125-passenger vessel may one cruise scenic Lake Taneycomo?

A. *Lake Queen*.

———◆———

Q. In what year did Joe Clark become the head soccer coach at Saint Louis University?

A. 1983.

———◆———

Q. Missouri Western State College's men's basketball team compiled what win/lose record for the 1990–91 season?

A. 23–8.

SCIENCE & NATURE

C H A P T E R   S I X

Q. The discovery of what type of toxic waste contamination focused national attention on Times Beach in January 1983?

A. Dioxin.

———◆———

Q. When was the last wild parakeet killed in Missouri?

A. 1905.

———◆———

Q. How tall was Ella Ewing, known as Missouri's Giantess?

A. Eight feet, four inches.

———◆———

Q. In 1843, what geologist discovered the sand deposits from which the glass manufacturing industry at Crystal City developed?

A. Forrest Shephard.

———◆———

Q. What geological formation near Thayer has been called the Little Grand Canyon?

A. Grand Gulf.

Q. Prior to World War I, what Smithton resident was the leading mule breeder in the nation?

A. Col. Louis M. Monsees.

———◆———

Q. At 1,772 feet above sea level, what is the highest point in Missouri?

A. Taumk Sauk Mountain.

———◆———

Q. Where did St. Joseph Lead Company construct the nation's largest lead smelter in 1890?

A. Herculaneum.

———◆———

Q. What animal accounts for 50 percent of all sheep losses by predators in Missouri?

A. Coyotes.

———◆———

Q. What cave near Noel features the fifty-four-foot Rimstone Dam?

A. Bluff Dweller's Cave.

———◆———

Q. As of 1990, what was the size of the average farm in Missouri?

A. 281 acres.

———◆———

Q. What historic winery, founded at Hermann in 1847, was at one time the nation's second-largest winery?

A. Stone Hill No. 1.

Q. More than 350 varieties of shrubs and trees, a fern grotto, and a rose garden are all part of what Columbia attraction?

A. Shelter Insurance Gardens.

———◆———

Q. What iron deposit was promoted in the 1830s as being the "largest and richest mass of iron on the globe"?

A. Iron Mountain.

———◆———

Q. In what year did President Truman declare Missouri a disaster area because of severe drought?

A. 1952.

———◆———

Q. In 1927, the state legislature designated what bird as the official state bird of Missouri?

A. Bluebird (*Sialia sialis*).

———◆———

Q. Under whose gubernatorial administration was the Missouri State Park system authorized?

A. Gov. Frank Gardner (1917–21).

———◆———

Q. What 400-acre park near Strafford features some 3,000 wild animals and rare birds?

A. Exotic Animal Paradise.

———◆———

Q. During the record year of 1975, how many head of beef cattle were in Missouri?

A. 2,759,000.

Q. What Kansas Citian invented the overhead trolley car in 1884?

A. John C. Henry.

———◆———

Q. Around 1870 what Chillicothe livery stable operator developed a world-famous horse liniment?

A. Earl Sawyer Sloan (Sloan's Liniment).

———◆———

Q. What Cornish miner first discovered lead in the Granby area in 1853?

A. William Foster.

———◆———

Q. Devil's Icebox Cave is an attraction of what state park in Boone County?

A. Rock Bridge State Park.

———◆———

Q. Founded in 1873, what is Missouri's largest winery?

A. Bardenheir's Wine Cellars.

———◆———

Q. What internationally famous black agricultural chemist and educator was born near Diamond around 1864?

A. George Washington Carver.

———◆———

Q. Where in Missouri is a museum honoring the American saddle horse?

A. Mexico.

Q. What Arrow Rock physician of the 1800s helped pioneer the use of quinine for the treatment of malaria?

A. Dr. John Sappington.

———◆———

Q. In the 1850s Missouri farmers in the prairie regions began planting what type of tree for hedgerows?

A. Osage orange.

———◆———

Q. Who plowed up a hunk of lead in his cornfield in 1873 that started a mining boom in Jasper County?

A. John C. Webb.

———◆———

Q. Averaging some 600 million gallons per day, what is the third-largest spring in the nation?

A. Big Spring.

———◆———

Q. What was the state's recorded precipitation for the drought year of 1901?

A. 25.28 inches.

———◆———

Q. Situated between Gravois Mills and Versailles, what is the largest cavern in the Lake of the Ozarks area?

A. Jacob's Cave.

———◆———

Q. Which county leads the state in the production of tobacco?

A. Platte.

Q. What Missouri winery is situated in downtown Blue Springs?

A. Spring Creek Winery.

Q. The Mississippi River at one time flowed west of what predominant geological feature in the southeastern part of the state?

A. Crowley's Ridge.

Q. In what year was the last wild buffalo seen in Missouri?

A. 1850.

Q. Missouri's wool industry peaked in 1942 with how many pounds of production?

A. 11,052,000.

Q. More than one hundred bald eagles and one of the largest concentrations of Canada geese in North America are attracted each winter to what wildlife center?

A. Swan Lake National Wildlife Refuge near Brookfield.

Q. With a wing span of up to fifty-five inches, what is the largest variety of owl found in Missouri?

A. Great Horned Owl.

Q. What community situated near the Warren and St. Charles county line was a noted tobacco manufacturing center during the 1870s?

A. Wentzville.

Q. During its boom days, what St. Francois County mining town was called the Lead Capital of the World?

A. Flat Rock.

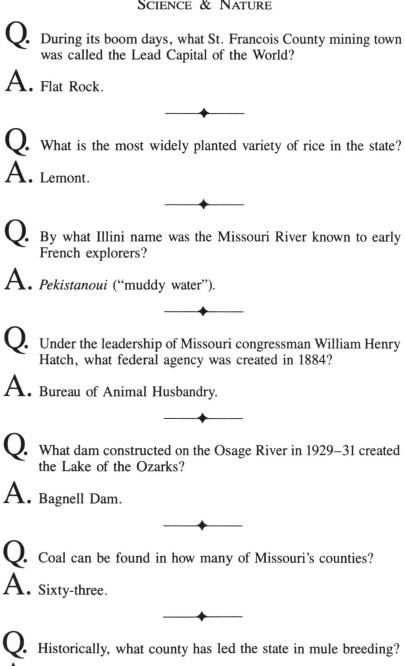

Q. What is the most widely planted variety of rice in the state?

A. Lemont.

Q. By what Illini name was the Missouri River known to early French explorers?

A. *Pekistanoui* ("muddy water").

Q. Under the leadership of Missouri congressman William Henry Hatch, what federal agency was created in 1884?

A. Bureau of Animal Husbandry.

Q. What dam constructed on the Osage River in 1929–31 created the Lake of the Ozarks?

A. Bagnell Dam.

Q. Coal can be found in how many of Missouri's counties?

A. Sixty-three.

Q. Historically, what county has led the state in mule breeding?

A. Callaway.

Q. What company manufacturing fire-clay products was founded at Mexico in 1910?

A. A. P. Green Brick Company.

———◆———

Q. How many raccoon pelts were harvested and registered by the Missouri fur industry during the 1986–87 season?

A. 229,908 pelts.

———◆———

Q. Who began publishing the *American Grape Culturist* at St. Louis in 1868?

A. George Hussmann.

———◆———

Q. What experimental and research cave facility is situated near Protem?

A. Ozark Underground Laboratory.

———◆———

Q. What county led the state in corn production in 1990, with 12,320,000 bushels?

A. Atchison County.

———◆———

Q. What type of bears appear on the Missouri state flag?

A. Grizzly.

———◆———

Q. Where may the nation's largest persimmon tree be seen?

A. Big Oak Tree State Park.

Q. The Current River receives approximately how many gallons of water daily from the Jack's Fork tributary?

A. 120 million.

———————◆———————

Q. What is the top fruit cash crop in Missouri?

A. Apples.

———————◆———————

Q. When erected in 1887 where was the largest sawmill in the state?

A. Grandin.

———————◆———————

Q. Formerly known as Big Salt Petre Cave and McDowell's Cave, Mark Twain Cave was discovered in the winter of 1819–20 by what hunter?

A. Jack Sims.

———————◆———————

Q. The wines of what Missouri vineyard are named for the streams in Crawford County?

A. Peaceful Bend Vineyard.

———————◆———————

Q. What type of manufactured goods from the Shelby County community of Bethel took first place at the New York World's Fair of 1858?

A. Buckskin gloves.

———————◆———————

Q. Where did B. G. Brown and Thomas Allen open stone quarries in 1868?

A. Graniteville.

Q. What three types of poisonous snakes are found in Missouri?

A. Copperhead, cottonmouth, and rattlesnake.

———◆———

Q. Reported at both Lamar and Warsaw, what has been the highest recorded temperature in the state?

A. 118 degrees Fahrenheit.

———◆———

Q. Where does Missouri rank nationally in the production of barite?

A. First.

———◆———

Q. Which Missouri cave is known for a spectacular twenty-story main chamber and a waterfall some five hundred feet below the surface?

A. Marvel Cave.

———◆———

Q. At present, approximately what percentage of Missouri is forested?

A. 34.5 percent.

———◆———

Q. A 625-acre oxbow lake is the central attraction of what state park in Holt County?

A. Big Lake State Park.

———◆———

Q. Excluding alfalfa, where does Missouri rank nationally in hay production?

A. Second.

Q. Between 1798 and 1816 how many tons of lead were smelted in the Potosi area?

A. 4,680.

———◆———

Q. What is the estimated Richter Scale measurement for the New Madrid earthquake of 1811–12?

A. 8.7, compared with 8.3 for the San Francisco quake of 1906.

———◆———

Q. In the 1920s what Houston druggist attempted to establish an electric interurban railway between Houston and Rolla?

A. Dr. P. A. Harrington.

———◆———

Q. Who discovered coal in Macon County in 1860 while digging a well near Bevier?

A. Alex Rector.

———◆———

Q. Approximately one-third of the total population of what endangered bat lives in Missouri?

A. Indiana bat.

———◆———

Q. What Missouri state park is situated in a reclaimed strip-mining area and features seven strip-pit lakes?

A. Finger Lakes State Park.

———◆———

Q. What is America's oldest national fish hatchery, established in 1888?

A. Neosho National Fish Hatchery.

Q. What limestone formation is the most widely quarried in the state?

A. Burlington.

———◆———

Q. What two types of vultures are found in Missouri?

A. Black and turkey.

———◆———

Q. After many years of controversy and protests, what Missouri power plant was completed in December 1984?

A. Callaway Nuclear Power Plant.

———◆———

Q. In what year was the last passenger pigeon reported in the state?

A. 1890.

———◆———

Q. Missouri ranks seventh in the nation in the production of what variety of grape?

A. Concord.

———◆———

Q. Traces of what metal in glacial deposits created a mild boom in the New Cambria area in 1875?

A. Gold.

———◆———

Q. What reclamation endeavor in the Boot Heel region during the early twentieth century greatly altered the area's environment?

A. The Little River Drainage Project.

Q. Civil War Cave near Ozark is locally known by what name?

A. Smallin's Cave.

———◆———

Q. What was the value of lumber production in Missouri in 1860?

A. $9 million.

———◆———

Q. What iron furnace opened near Potosi in 1826?

A. Springfield Iron Furnace and Forge.

———◆———

Q. The eighty-acre Kansas City Zoo is situated in what park?

A. Swope Park.

———◆———

Q. Since 1869 Seneca has been known for the mining and processing of what material used as a polishing compound, manufacturing additive, and component in high-grade filters?

A. Tripoli.

———◆———

Q. In what year was Lake Wappapello completed?

A. 1941.

———◆———

Q. The large ancient Indian earthwork in Van Meter State Park is locally known by what name?

A. Old Fort.

Q. What is the largest game bird found in Missouri?

A. Wild turkey.

———◆———

Q. The viticultural experiments of Herschel Gray at Chestnut Ridge led to the establishment of what winery?

A. Ozark Vineyard and Winery.

———◆———

Q. How many residents were killed in Marshfield by tornadoes which struck in 1878 and 1880?

A. Eighty-seven.

———◆———

Q. Who established the Missouri School for the Blind in St. Louis in 1851?

A. Eli W. Whalen.

———◆———

Q. What Ste. Genevieve-born hydrographer was the first to survey systematically the Pacific coast?

A. William Pope McArthur.

———◆———

Q. The St. Louis Zoological Park is home to how many animals?

A. More than 2,800.

———◆———

Q. What percentage of Missouri's electricity is produced by coal?

A. About 80 percent.

Q. How many acres of land are included in Mark Twain National Forest?

A. Approximately 1.5 million.

———◆———

Q. What St. Joseph museum gives visitors an overview of some 400 years of psychiatric treatment methods?

A. State Hospital Psychiatric Museum.

———◆———

Q. What state park is centered on Missouri's fourth-largest spring?

A. Bennett Spring State Park.

———◆———

Q. What white grape variety was developed by Judge Samuel Miller of Bluffton in the 1860s?

A. Martha.

———◆———

Q. In 1850, Missouri produced how many barrels of beer?

A. 172,570.

———◆———

Q. What was declared the state flower of Missouri in 1923?

A. Hawthorn *(Crataegus mollis)*.

———◆———

Q. Who established Missouri's first shot tower in 1809 at Herculaneum?

A. J. N. Maclot.

Q. What cave near Springfield offers jeep tours and stage shows?

A. Fantastic Caverns.

Q. During the 1869–70 processing season, how many hogs were slaughtered and processed at Alexandria?

A. 42,557.

Q. In 1792, what beneficial insect was introduced into Missouri?

A. Honeybee.

Q. Who opened a salt works at Randolph Springs in 1823?

A. Dr. William Fort.

Q. What two types of squirrels are most common in Missouri?

A. Eastern gray and fox.

Q. The farms of Dunklin County lead the state in the production of what commodity?

A. Cotton.

Q. In 1850, what was the most productive lead mine in the Neosho area?

A. Mosely, Oldham & Company.

Q. Who first explored Fairy Cave near Reeds Spring in 1896?

A. Truman S. Powell.

———◆———

Q. What St. Louis radio station was the first to broadcast from a moving train?

A. KSD.

———◆———

Q. In 1924 where did Springfield rank nationally in the production of churned butter?

A. Fourth.

———◆———

Q. When did the first shock of the gigantic 1811–12 New Madrid earthquake occur?

A. 2:00 A.M., December 16, 1811.

———◆———

Q. For what price were commercially hunted ruffed grouse selling in St. Louis in 1878?

A. $2.75 to $3.00 per dozen.

———◆———

Q. What is the most widely planted public variety of soybean in the state?

A. Williams.

———◆———

Q. In a move to improve dairy stock in the state, who organized the first Missouri Dairy Club at Carthage in 1916?

A. E. G. Bennett.

Q. Missouri's lowest point, where the St. Francis River exits the state, is at what elevation?

A. 245 feet above sea level.

———◆———

Q. What thirty-nine-acre nature preserve is at Gladstone?

A. Maple Woods Natural Area.

———◆———

Q. Listed as a National Historic Landmark, what is the oldest botanical garden in the nation?

A. Missouri Botanical Garden, St. Louis.

———◆———

Q. What state park near Graniteville features unique geological formations?

A. Elephant Rocks State Park.

———◆———

Q. From 1881 to 1921 how many blast furnaces operated at Sligo?

A. Seven.

———◆———

Q. What cooperative creamery was established in Lafayette County in 1892?

A. Concordia Creamery Company.

———◆———

Q. Over its approximate 160-mile length, what is the average fall per mile of the Current River?

A. Seven feet.

Q. What 807-acre botanical garden was established at Kingsville in 1984?

A. Powell Gardens.

———◆———

Q. In 1902, what Atchison County farmer owned and operated the largest corn farm in the world, consisting of some 30,000 acres?

A. David Rankin.

———◆———

Q. What oil strike was made in Atchison County in 1942?
A. Tarkio Pool.

———◆———

Q. Dunklin, New Madrid, Pemiscot, and Stoddard counties lead the state in the production of what grain crop?

A. Wheat.

———◆———

Q. What winery near Lone Jack features wine produced from Seyval Blanc, Villard Blanc, Chancellor, and Concord grapes?

A. Bynum Winery.

———◆———

Q. On February 13, 1905, what record low temperature for the state was recorded at Warsaw?

A. Minus 40 degrees Fahrenheit.

———◆———

Q. In what year were the first stockyards built in Kansas City?
A. 1870.

Q. What natural cause ignited three barrels of liquor at a log hotel in Oregon on July 8, 1851, killing six patrons?

A. Lightning.

———◆———

Q. An important deposit of what type of material was discovered at Mexico shortly after 1900?

A. Fire clay.

———◆———

Q. Where does Missouri rank nationally in the number of caves open for commercial viewing?

A. First (with twenty-six).

———◆———

Q. Approximately how much breeding area for prairie chickens remains in Missouri?

A. 700 square miles.

———◆———

Q. For what purpose is most of the corn grown in the state used?

A. Livestock feed.

———◆———

Q. What is the largest river in the state north of the Missouri River?

A. The Grand.

———◆———

Q. A state record was set in 1944 with what egg production figure?

A. 3,052,000,000.

Q. In what county was the state's first oil well drilled in the 1860s?

A. Jackson.

———◆———

Q. Situated in the heart of the old Lead Belt, what is the second-largest state park in Missouri?

A. St. Joe State Park.

———◆———

Q. Table Rock Lake covers how many acres?

A. 53,300.

———◆———

Q. The watershed of the area around Cedar Gap, which feeds Gasconada River to the north and White River to the south, is known by what name?

A. Ozark Divide.

———◆———

Q. What cavern near Cassville is said to contain the largest variety of formations in the nation?

A. Crystal Caverns.

———◆———

Q. Approximately how many commercial bee colonies are there in the state?

A. 30,000.

———◆———

Q. Where in Springfield may more than 400 specimens of wildlife be seen?

A. Dickerson Park Zoo.

Q. Impounded in 1913, what lake today stretches between Table Rock Lake and Bull Shoals Lake?

A. Lake Taneycomo.

———◆———

Q. What two counties lead the state in the production of hogs and pigs?

A. Lafayette and Osage.

———◆———

Q. From the waters in what cavern was a thirty-nine-foot-long Indian dugout canoe retrieved in 1937?

A. Keener Cave.

———◆———

Q. How many gallons of whiskey were produced in Missouri in 1840?

A. Approximately one-half million.

———◆———

Q. Iron ore from Pilot Knob and Iron Mountain was smelted at what Mississippi River town until 1882?

A. Kimmswick.

———◆———

Q. Lewis and Clark State Park is situated on the southern edge of what lake?

A. Sugar Lake.

———◆———

Q. What type of coal is mined in Missouri?

A. Bituminous.

Q. The damming of what river created the Lake of the Ozarks?

A. The Osage.

———◆———

Q. What strain of hunting dog was developed at Monroe City?

A. Spalding-Norris foxhound.

———◆———

Q. In 1938, what 5,329-acre tract in northern Pettis County was opened by the federal government for the resettlement of farmers who had been devastated by the Depression?

A. Osage Farms.

———◆———

Q. What Hannibal lawyer and U.S. congressman is known as the "father of agricultural experiment stations"?

A. William Henry Hatch.

———◆———

Q. In the early 1800s what was the approximate annual production of lead at Mine La Motte?

A. 300,000 pounds.

———◆———

Q. Who was Missouri's first industrialist?

A. Moses Austin.

———◆———

Q. What vineyard south of Cassville features native wild and hybrid grapes of Missouri?

A. Herman Jaeger Memorial Vineyard.

Q. When it was built in 1874, the nation's largest observatory west of the Mississippi River was constructed in what town?

A. Glasgow.

Q. At what depth did early miners in the Grandy area find deposits of lead and zinc?

A. Ten to seventy-five feet.

Q. What river flows through Bennett Spring State Park?

A. Niangua River.

Q. Though now restored to a large statewide population, white-tailed deer had been reduced to what small number in 1937?

A. About 2,000.

Q. In 1840, how many pounds of tobacco were produced in the state?

A. 9,067,913 pounds.

Q. Silica or industrial sand, which is mined in eastern Missouri, comes from what Ordovician deposit?

A. St. Peter Sandstone.

Q. What Mount Airy-born medical educator headed the first bacteriological laboratory in the nation?

A. Victor Clarence Vaughan.

Q. In 1902, J. N. Alsop of Jackson developed an electrical process to bleach what food product?

A. Flour.

———◆———

Q. During the Boer War what Lancaster mule dealer received large contracts from the South African government?

A. Col. William P. Hall.

———◆———

Q. What mining company was incorporated at Bonne Terre in 1864?

A. St. Joseph Lead Company.

———◆———

Q. In what year did James Stark establish the world-famous Stark Brothers Nursery in Pike County?

A. 1816.

———◆———

Q. How many catfish fingerlings were sold by Missouri hatcheries in 1990?

A. 5,731,000.

———◆———

Q. The Chicago and Alton Railroad Bridge, erected across the Missouri River at Glasgow in 1878–79, became the world's first railway bridge to be constructed entirely of what material?

A. Steel.

———◆———

Q. Butler County ranks first in the state in the production of what grain crop?

A. Rice.

Q. What percentage of the national population of the endangered gray bat is found in Missouri?

A. About 20 percent.

———◆———

Q. How many springs in the Missouri Ozarks have an average daily flow of more than 24 million gallons?

A. Fifteen.

———◆———

Q. In 1892, what physician and researcher founded the American School of Osteopathy at Kirksville?

A. Dr. Andrew Taylor Still.

———◆———

Q. The regular mining of what metal was started in Shannon County around 1837?

A. Copper.

———◆———

Q. The bones of musk ox, woolly mammoth, and giant bison have been found in what commercial cave near Rocheport?

A. Boone Cave.

———◆———

Q. What winery was founded at Cuba in 1980?

A. Mount Pleasant Winery-Abbey.

———◆———

Q. Where is the only public planetarium in the Kansas City metropolitan area?

A. Kansas City Museum.

Q. In 1937 what was the estimated number of ruffed grouse left in Missouri?

A. Fewer than 100.

———◆———

Q. What St. Louis museum displays the world's largest collection of locomotives?

A. National Museum of Transportation.

———◆———

Q. During the 1850s for what business venture did W. N. Marshall propose that a large lake be created from the springs at Boon's Lick?

A. Raising of oysters and saltwater fish.

———◆———

Q. Where did the marble used in Macy's department store in New York city come from?

A. Carthage.

———◆———

Q. The Sam Hildebrand Cave is on what river in northern St. Francois County?

A. The Big River.

———◆———

Q. About 1880 what physician constructed a sanatorium, the Mineral Springs Hotel, at Mooresville?

A. Dr. Theophilus Fish.

———◆———

Q. In what year did the Harry S Truman Reservoir begin to fill?

A. 1978.

Q. The site of the Oronogo Circle Mine north of Webb City, which produced lead and zinc ore worth some $30 million, is said to have been purchased for what amount in 1854?

A. Fifty dollars.

━━━━━◆━━━━━

Q. How many caves are situated in Meramec State Park?

A. Twenty.

━━━━━◆━━━━━

Q. What is Missouri's largest state park, which covers 17,213 acres?

A. Lake of the Ozarks State Park.

━━━━━◆━━━━━

Q. Approximately what percentage of public water systems in Missouri rely on ground water as their primary source?

A. 60 percent.

━━━━━◆━━━━━

Q. The Missouri River, which joins the Mississippi just north of St. Louis, pours an average of how many cubic feet of water per second into the Mississippi?

A. 69,300.

━━━━━◆━━━━━

Q. In 1937, what state agency was created to assist in the management, preservation, and restoration of wildlife?

A. Missouri Department of Conservation.

━━━━━◆━━━━━

Q. Though seldom seen south of Alaska, what type of bird delighted watchers in the West Alton area in January 1992?

A. Ross's gull (*Rhodostethia rosea*).

Q. Presentations, films, and demonstrations about good dental hygiene are all a part of what St. Louis attraction?

A. Dental Health Theater.

———◆———

Q. Where is Wilderness Safari, featuring a variety of exotic animals and birds?

A. Branson.

———◆———

Q. Measuring some seventy-five miles in length, what is the largest coal field in the state?

A. Bevier Coal Field.

———◆———

Q. Who established the Kingsbury Orchards in Howard County in 1871?

A. R. T. Kingsbury.

———◆———

Q. In 1939, a treatment facility was opened in Rolla for what highly contagious chronic disease of the eyelids?

A. Trachoma.

———◆———

Q. What Missouri River town was recognized at the 1853 New York State Fair as producing the finest Catawba wine west of the Mississippi River?

A. Hermann.

———◆———

Q. On June 22, 1947, how many inches of rain fell at Holt in forty-two minutes?

A. Twelve inches.

Q. The rock debris deposited by ancient glaciers in the northern half of the state is known by what term?

A. Drift.

———◆———

Q. By the mid-1930s how many river otters were believed to exist in the state?

A. About seventy.

———◆———

Q. Corn is grown on what percentage of Missouri farms?

A. 50 percent.

———◆———

Q. Lead and zinc mining had ceased in southwest Missouri by what year?

A. 1957.

———◆———

Q. What cave near Noel was reportedly used during the Civil War as an ammunition dump?

A. Ozark Wonder Cave.

———◆———

Q. The McDonnell Star Theater and Monsanto Science Park are two of the features of what St. Louis attraction?

A. St. Louis Science Center.

———◆———

Q. How many springs in Montauk State Park form the headwaters of the Current River?

A. Seven.

Q. What was Missouri's peak year for milk production?

A. 1954.

———◆———

Q. What is the largest trout hatchery in the state?

A. Shepherd of the Hills Trout Hatchery in Branson.

———◆———

Q. What was the record number of rattlesnakes killed at Clarksville during one of the town's annual spring hunts?

A. 9,000.

———◆———

Q. Missouri rocks, minerals, and mining machinery are featured at what Joplin museum?

A. Tri-State Mineral Museum.

———◆———

Q. The nation's first federally designated viticultural area was situated around what town?

A. Augusta.

———◆———

Q. What was the percentage of iron in the ore that was mined from Iron Mountain?

A. 50 to 60 percent.

———◆———

Q. What county had the largest cattle population in the state in 1992, with 106,500 head?

A. Lawrence.

Q. What marsh and wildlife management area is near Ashburn?

A. Ted Shanks Wildlife Area.

———◆———

Q. How many tons of lead were produced in 1976 from the New Lead Belt in Iron and Reynolds counties, making it the world's leader for a single production district?

A. Approximately one-half million.

———◆———

Q. Where may one see Thomas Edison's restored dynamo, used in the first demonstration of incandescent lighting west of the Mississippi?

A. Electrical Engineering Building, University of Missouri-Columbia.

———◆———

Q. What Newton County viticulturalist received the French Legion of Honor medal for his help in restoring France's wine vineyards that were devastated by phylloxera?

A. Herman Jaeger.

———◆———

Q. How many pounds of butter were produced in Missouri in 1900?

A. Almost 47 million pounds.

———◆———

Q. Canyon-like gaps along the Black River in Lester County are known by what term?

A. Shut-ins.

———◆———

Q. Born of slave parents on a farm near Diamond, George Washington Carver made more than 300 products from what legume?

A. Peanut.

Q. The twenty-seven mineral springs in the state fall into what three major mineral types?

A. Salt, sulphur, and iron.

———◆———

Q. During Missouri's unusually wet year of 1927 what was the recorded amount of precipitation?

A. 55.06 inches.

———◆———

Q. What commercial cave is situated near Stanton?

A. Meramec Caverns.

———◆———

Q. In 1914, what St. Louis firm was appointed by the federal government to dress and dye all seal skins from Alaska?

A. Fouke Fur Company.

———◆———

Q. Between 1894 and 1904 the lead and zinc mines around Webb City produced minerals worth approximately how much?

A. $23 million.

———◆———

Q. Measuring up to fifteen inches in length, what is the largest variety of woodpecker found in Missouri?

A. Pileated woodpecker.

———◆———

Q. In 1955, the state legislature designated what tree as the official state tree of Missouri?

A. Flowering dogwood (*Cornus florida*).

Ernie Couch and his wife, Jill, own and operate Consultx, a support firm for the publishing industry with specialties in advertising and graphic design. Together they compiled fourteen other trivia books.